DIVE WITHIN

DIVE WITHIN

Bhupendra Singh Rathore

"Master of Transformational Breakthroughs"

PARTRIDGE

A Penguin Random House Company

To order additional copies of this book, contact
Partridge India
000 800 10062 62
www.partridgepublishing.com/india
orders.india@partridgepublishing.com

CONTENTS

ACKNOWLEDGEMENTS

Every journey starts with some excitement and comes to an end. Few journeys are short and some longer. The best part about each journey is that—you meet many wonderful people and spend time with them. Some help you and show you the way ahead, some decide to walk with you till you reach the destination safely, some motivate you while you are moving towards the finishing point, some give you joy and happiness, some remain silent, still end up playing a powerful role in making your journey fruitful and exciting!

Writing this book was also a journey for me, full of learning, excitement, life and challenges. It became wonderful as many people helped, supported and guided me during the course of this journey.

I would like to express my gratitude to all my teachers and trainers whom I met during the past 30 years of my life. Their contribution to my life as well as in shaping this book has indeed been amazing. *Majority of the thoughts* captured in this book are inspired by them and learnt through them. They have shown me the path and I kept walking on it.

I would like to acknowledge the significant role which my family has played in helping me practice everything which I share here in this book.

The inspiration to write this book came from my father "Mr Raghuveer Singh Rathore" and my wife *'Ms. Ritambhara Ranawat'* who pushed me beyond my limits to complete it. They helped me discover the reason for writing a book. They also pushed me to propel it forward with great enthusiasm to all you readers.

My entire team and my business partner 'Mr. *Pavan Rathore'* also helped me in many subtle ways to complete this book.

My special thanks to *'Ms. Devasmita Dey Chowdhary'* who kept herself fully involved in completion of this book. Her valuable suggestions, guidance and support got the best out of me. She contributed a lot of her time & efforts in researching, re-reading and amending the entire script of this book, which are truly appreciative.

A huge credit for writing this book also goes to all those people who have attended my sessions and seminars, as many of the insights have come from questions which they asked in my journey, to find, discover and help answer them.

Love to All!

"Tring-Tring"

Hey 'Ritu!' what a coincidence . . . . I was just thinking about you!

Or

Cheez! 'I had this strong feeling, that I would lose my purse today' I just saw it coming . . . and I did lose it!

Tell me? How many of us have come across such situations? Probably everybody and maybe many number of times too. In fact it's so common that it does not surprise us anymore.

Murphy's Law—'When something has to go wrong, it will go wrong',

The matching of the wavelength with the other person,

The positive vibes,

The negative vibes . . .

Such incidents have become part of our everyday lives. We have accepted them as a natural phenomenon. Not many of us have asked this question "why such things happen?" We all dismiss such situations as 'coincidence' or 'rotten luck'. We have never really thought beyond that. But, what if these things are not merely 'coincidences' or 'rotten luck' but something that's been brought into our lives by our thoughts and immense will power?

Welcome to the Most Powerful World—Your Mind

Let's **"Dive Within"** to unleash your "Mind Power"

"Have you ever heard that in a car or bus accident
all travellers died but a 1 year old baby miraculously
survived?"

"A person to whom the doctors declared that he won't
live for more than 3 days survives over 30 years and
grows strong miraculously."

"You also are aware of many such incidents in this
world which even science and all scientists can't explain?

A huge examination and you prepare for only 25% of
the question-answers and miraculously you get most
questions from that 25% . . .

Are they not miracles?

Oh yes! They are . . . . miracles do happen!

Miracles happen for those who are focused. Who vibrate with positive energy and are enthusiastic. Who give their best and think big.

I would say a "miracle" is an occurrence of that event which seems almost impossible but then it happens. Miracle for me is also something which I dreamt of and didn't work for it and yet it became my reality . . . . almost like a magic!

The best part is that God has gifted us with an amazing power of creating magic. It is all mystical for someone who doesn't know the trick behind the magic. But ask a magician, and he will tell you exactly how it works. And there is perfect logic to it, planning down to the last millisecond, precise timing as well as a valid scientific explanation . . . right? Unfortunately most of us are witnessing our own lives as spectators in spite of having the power to be a magician.

Do you want to discover the magician in you? Yes, you don't need to create a magician inside you, as you already have one whose powers are not even known to you.

So read on and we will break through some of these magical bricks with our inbuilt magician's hat—the mind—after we say the magical word. No, it's not abra-ka-dabra. This time let's try something different. Let's say 'Tathastu'.

TATHASTU

Tathastu loosely translates into 'so-be-it' or 'let your wish be granted'.

But I am sure you have the question—who says TATHASTU? Who makes our wish come true? Where is the magician's hat and wand?

The answer to all these questions is very simple—It's our Mind. The ultimate of all magicians, the Superpower!

You must have heard of the great sages and monks who walked through fire and on water. The dark lonely depths of the Himalayas are still said to be home for sages mediating through decades without food and water and also defying death! There are amazing visuals of people pulling a train with their teeth, holding their breath while a truck rolls over their chest, and bending an iron rod with the glare of their eyes! Science of yesteryears has called it all bullshit and as I write it, I am still compelled to put an exclamation sign at the end of the sentence. Actually I shouldn't, because today this very science has hacked into its secret and acknowledged it to be true and have backed it up with relevant scientific proofs. **Quantum Physics** is the stream of scientific studies that is delving into the science behind this humungous power of the mind and is making progress in leaps and bounds.

Physics tells us that this whole universe is a huge magnet which has an extensive magnetic field and we, a power house of magnetic bodies.

What we think, say, dream and desire has a magnetic strength to it and connects with the greater magnetic wavelength of the universe. This magnetic strength has signals which contain electrons, protons and neutrons. Electrons, protons and neutrons are invisible to naked eyes but we can view them under a powerful microscope. They are real bodies even though we cannot see them. These bodies are released in the atmosphere by us. These then vibrate with the combined energy of the electrons, protons and neutrons of the same wavelength of the universe and bring home the wish or materialize the thought—good or bad.

This means that the signals of a good thought will attract and combine with similar wavelength of the universe and a bad thought will attract and combine with like wavelength from the universe. And both will bring home the results of their individual thoughts. So now can we understand, a little scientifically, the reason behind the entire hullabaloo about 'positive thoughts'?

Our Universe has got the magical force that gives you anything you want—happiness, health, wealth . . . anything! It's the natural law of the universe. It's the 'LAW OF ATTRACTION'. If I really get down to the crux of this law then it can be summarized in few a pointers

'Believe in yourself as you are the part of God and God is nothing but you'

'Do what you love to do and be joyful'

'Take Massive leaps of faiths'

LAW OF ATTRACTION is always in force, even when we are asleep, and not consciously aware of it. Through one of my most powerful workshops 'IGNITING THE SPARK' year after year I have tried to reach out to as many people as possible to make them aware of this very LAW OF ATTRACTION and the power of the mind through which this law works. There are step-by-step methods of using this Law and a scientific explanation to each of these steps to accredit their validation. Through this book you will be aware of the working of this machine—called Mind, and hence will be able to use it better and to its fullest advantage.

Why am I doing this? Or why, you may ask, have I picked this up as my profession?

This is because in an endeavour to give some meaning and direction to my life, I decided to go through this learning myself. There was a point of time in my life when I was not sure of my future. I was directionless. I really did not know what I wanted to do. I wanted to achieve something, but what that 'something' was I did not know. My mind was a junkyard of unrelated thoughts, useless and meaningless and I could not shift through them effectively. Since I decided not to tout the line of the general, I was labelled incompetent, useless, radar less, and someone who will not make it in his life. I believed in all these labels, but did not believe in myself. I stumbled. Every time I saw someone more successful than me, I got uncomfortable. I saw him as a huge superior being and thought it impossible for me to do anything like him.

I never liked to do things which were challenging as I had a fear of failure. In order to save myself I designed an escape route—never to participate in any competition or any school or college event. Wow! . . . what a shortcut it was . . . . today when I look back I realize that had I continued following that shortcut, then I would have been responsible for the murder of the REAL ME.

There were things I really wanted to do but every time I tried my hand at something I always failed. It was of course, someone else's fault; always someone else, or something else, but never me. And then there were those two big words that we all take shelter in from time to time—LUCK and FATE. I was not aware of the things I knew. What I didn't know could have filled up a book the size of a sky scraper!

When I started to seek training, it was initially to improve my English. Then in a seemingly incoherent chain of events, one training automatically led to the other till I reached my zenith. I was made to realize, through these sessions and by my guru (teacher) that **everything** that we are searching for **is within us**, in our subconscious mind. No outside force is responsible for our failure or success, sadness or happiness, goodness or badness. The entire onus is on us.

One of my Gurus says it very nicely—**"All I need, is within me now".** **And after going through a lot of practical life experiences, I can say it with a great confidence that—'YES! All I really need is within** me NOW'. I am sure by the time you reach the last line of this book; you will also start believing in the same . . .

So let's 'Dive Within'. For this very knowledge changed my life, gave me the required direction till I was burning to share it. I wanted to reach out to as many people as possible and share it with them, 'the logic behind the magic'

LAWS OF MIND

I am sure you might have come across many such situations where you had an intuition about something and that happened. I am also sure that many a times you didn't want someone to do a particular job and he did exactly what you didn't want him to do. You thought how stupid he is.

I would be very blunt in saying that it's you who is STUPID, not him. **This is because you have never understood—how your mind functions and how you attract majority of the things in your life.**

Analogy: *Mr. Golgappa went into the restaurant and ordered Pasta and chicken from the menu card. He ordered and then got busy talking to his clients. After 20 minutes when the waiter was about to serve him the dishes Mr. Golgappa said "I have never ordered this dish." Upon this, the waiter said, "Sir you have ordered this same dish. I have a written record." Mr. Golgappa said, "I ordered something else but definitely not chicken and pasta." The waiter was confused and there was a huge argument. The actual challenge here was that Mr. Golgappa had a short term memory loss, a medical condition and hence he forgot what he said. On top of this he did not know that he has this problem of losing his memory.*

Why I am sharing this with you is: we are in the restaurant called Universe and all the time we keep ordering something or the other from the catalogue of this universe. **How we order is not by asking, but by feeling, thinking, speaking and acting.** Right this moment, the way you are feeling is getting ordered from the catalogue of this universe and you will get more of it. But like Mr. Golgappa, we forget our own wish. A real time memory loss.

There is one more reason behind this memory loss—when we order from the universe, we never know how long it will take to get processed and that delay makes us forget whatever we have ordered. The challenging part is, very few people actually are aware of what they order. We do not discriminate with our thoughts and feelings. That's because we are not aware of the power of it!

There is one rule in every restaurant—and that is, you can change the order if they have not started working on it—so in the same way, you can cancel the order you placed in the Universe if you become aware of what you are ordering. Because the best part about the universe is that nothing happens instantly. It takes time to get the order processed.

To bring the awareness about how we order the things from the catalogue of this universe we will have to understand few laws of our own mind. This part plays a vital role in keeping us connected to this universe.

For the first time I learned the laws of the mind. 'Laws of the mind?' Does the mind follow laws? It felt strange in the beginning, for I thought that the mind was boundless. Well I was right! But even in its boundlessness it follows a law—

1. **Mind does not understand the words or the language. It only understands pictures.** That's why we remember things better when we see them.

   If I speak any word I am sure you are going to picturize it. Let's test it—"A person is carrying a bag on his shoulder, which is red in colour" Oh!!! . . . what happened? Did you read the sentence which I wrote or did you imagine a person carrying a red colour bag on his shoulder.

   Yes that's what your mind does and hence if you tell yourself "I don't want loan, I don't want negativity, I don't want problems": Guess what your mind does? It only visualizes loan, negativity and problem!

   "You are constantly ordering what your mind is visualizing and your heart is feeling"—BSR

   Be careful! If there is a negative visualization or a feeling which you don't want, you immediately need to do something to change it; else you are falling in the trap of this law of your mind. Take a Powerful Action, Sing a loud song, Speak to a friend who is positive or dance—Anything! But do something.

   All great leaders only focus on what they want and that's one of the biggest secret behind their success. Do you want to be the next success story—if yes, then take charge.

2. **Mind doesn't understand the difference between imagination and reality.** That's why we cry when we watch a movie. Horror movies terrify us for days on end, even though you tell yourself a thousand times that it was just a movie.

What happens to you when you have a fear in your mind? Fear gets created when you visualize something which has not yet happened or happened in the past but you don't want it to happen to you again.

Why does fear paralyze you?

The simple reason is because it's difficult for your subconscious mind to distinguish between imagination and reality. When you are scared all the negative possibilities run in your mind. Some are evoked from movies that we watched in the past, some from our great imaginative mind and then there are previous experiences to recall from and relate to. We all know they are not real, yet it feels so real that the real actions and reactions start happening in your body.

How many of you experience a nervous breakdown when you sit to write your examination? Too many of us go through that. Why? Because the thought of a probable failure paralyzes you and drives you nuts!

Around 3 months ago a house caught fire. A happy family of 4 was residing in that house. Both the kids and the mother were in the house at the time of fire and they were sleeping as it was late in the night. Somehow the lady got the courage and helped her kids to move out but she herself got stuck in there. She was screaming for help on top of her voice. People did their best to help her but the fire was getting worst. By the time fire brigade reached the place the lady had suffered severe burns and died. It was indeed a horrible scene.

Hello!! Wake up; whatever I told in the above paragraph was a lie. It was a lie. But without thinking whether it was true or false, your mind started to visualize the entire scene and I am sure you could imagine the house on fire, lady struggling to save her kids, screaming for help and burning in the fire. That's what your mind does. Now read the below paragraph

Imagine that there are 5000 people sitting in the auditorium. They all have come to hear you as you are one of the top speakers in the country. You are the one who has been behind the transformation of millions of lives. There goes a person on the stage to introduce you in the most amazing way and the moment you come on the stage all 5000 people welcome you with a standing round of applause. Wherever yours eyes can go—you see only people standing and clapping for you. The sounds of those claps are incredible and that's filling you with great joy and excitement. Now all the people sit down and you start sharing your wisdom with them. They are listening to you with amazing concentration and you are able to keep them on the edge of their seats. What an incredible moment. Visualize yourself speaking in the most powerful way. In the first row of this auditorium you can see your parents, brother, sister, spouse, kids and close friends and relatives. Once in a while you look at them and you can see that they have an amazing smile on their face while they see you speaking with such wonderful confidence and charm. Now your speech gets over and you again get a thundering round of applause from all the people. Seeing this success of yours, your parents have tears in their eyes. They come on the stage and give you a tight hug in front of this huge crowd. When this miraculous hug gets over, you can see there is a large queue of people who are eager to take your autograph.

WOW! Isn't it a powerful visualization? Yes it is. This time I am sure you could literally see yourself in front of 5000 people and could hear those claps and feel that hug which you got from your friends. I am sure you felt great after reading the last paragraph.

I just want to convey through these paragraphs that your mind is a brilliant connection making machine. The moment you give it a thought it connects the dots as per the existing, reprints with it and starts producing the images which looks real to it. It connects the dots so well and creates the pictures so well that it itself can't distinguish between what is real and what is fake.

Your mind is a great servant—if you make it see the right picture, it will always fire the right signals for your body to act and ultimately you will achieve what you want. That's why it's said that whatever you can create in your mind will always be achieved. That's why visualization plays an important role in your success.

Visualize what you want and then see the miracles in your life.

3. **Mind always likes effortlessness.** We always search for the easy way out. And here comes the theory of the calculation of pain and pleasure, which we will discuss later in the book.

How many times have you promised yourself to get up early in the morning and when the alarm bell rang you kept putting it on snooze and by the time you got up you were way too late?

Think about the time when someone pushed you to study or when you pushed yourself to study—how was your productivity compared to when you really felt like studying.

Your productivity was way higher when you wanted to rather than when you pushed or were pushed to study.

Ever wondered why these things happen?

Such things happen because your mind doesn't really want to work hard. Mind is like a stubborn kid. So we cannot really force it to perform. Though we can sometimes bribe it and manipulate it.

You also might have felt that when you were passionate for something you lost track of time, your appetite etc. That is the time you work tirelessly and you feel great about it. When you follow your passion you work at your best. Have you ever thought—Why?

Because when your mind likes to do something, it doesn't get tired and it doesn't perceive it as a forceful or hard task. It cooperates and loves what you are doing.

If you are in a job which you don't like and you have no other option but to stick to it then my suggestion to you is: don't push yourself to perform. The more you push the more you will get tired and will start losing hope. Instead start visualizing the best possible outcome. Start becoming creative at your work. After every hour or so do something which can fill you with positive energy and excite you. It can be as simple as talking to a friend who is interesting or reading a page of comic book. Be grateful about what you have, as many don't even have that bit. Appreciate yourself. Soon you will see that the job, which you don't like, will start being less painful for you and your mind will find some ways to get aligned with it or will help you getting something which excites you.

The rule of thumb is, by forcing your mind you will always receive something which you will never be able to appreciate and admire as your mind perceives a lot of efforts in doing that and hence will resist.

4. **It acts faster on other's commands.** Somehow that has been proven true. We refuse to listen to ourselves easily. Your mind may at times not take commands given by you but it always receives and reciprocates the commands of others faster. This is the reason why we learn faster when people teach us rather than we read and understand for ourselves.

As per the mythological stories lord Hanuman was one of the most powerful deities. His powers were unlimited. When he was a kid he jumped and took the entire sun in his mouth. He could destroy anyone or anything with just one powerful punch. But due to some curse he forgot all his powers. When lord Rama had to send a messenger to give Ravan a warning and get the information about Sita, he was disappointed as there was no one in his entire team who could cross the entire sea. At that point Jamwant reminded lord Hanuman about his powers and about his childhood activities. The moment lord Hanuman became aware of his powers he stood up and with one jump crossed the entire sea and killed many devils like—Sursa, Sinhini, Lankini, Akshaykumar etc.

We all want a "Jamwant" in our life who can remind us about our own powers as we are powerful beyond measures. Probably that's the reason—all great CEO's, Leaders, Star Sports people always have their coaches who guide them, motivate them and remind them about their unlimited powers.

The unfortunate thing is that the reverse is also true. When someone tells us about our weaknesses, faults or criticizes us, mind acts on those commands as well. That's why when someone asks me how to stay positive throughout one's life—I suggest **"Surround yourself with positive people and stay away from negative people."**

5. **Whatever a human mind can conceive, it can achieve.** That is the ultimate truth!

Your mind is like that powerful magnet which has the power to attract whatever it wants. Yes it's a fact.

"If you leave your home to go to 'New Delhi', you are only going to reach there but not to New York. You will reach New York only when you decide to go there."

Wherever you have reached or whatever you have achieved will all depend upon what you think and how you act upon your thoughts.

If you look around you will find that people often talk about earning handsome salary which means earning Rs 30000 INR to 100000 INR and most of them, after a lot of hard work and lot of time, are able to reach, where they dreamt of. In the same society you will find some people who honed their dreams about a luxurious life and earning in millions, also get what they dreamt of.

The law of life is whatever your mind thinks repeatedly with the same intensity, it starts believing in that after a point of time and hence does everything possible to turn it into your reality.

I often share with people that why don't they visualize something big, because the fact is whether you visualize big or small, negative or positive—the same amount of energy is going to get consumed, in fact the negative visualization will consume more energy.

That's why many a times you have heard—Think big!—there is definitely some logic behind it.

6. **Mind Loves Balance**—the biggest fact.

Imbalance is not possible in nature and in the universe. The law of universe says that this world will never have less energy or more energy. It will always have the same energy as it had on the day of its creation. Your very existence is a natural process and your subconscious mind works just in sync with this nature. It never goes out of sync. If your conscious mind affects this balance then your subconscious mind will do everything possible to bring that balance again.

There is no way your mind is going to accept the imbalance. If you look at the world and life around, then you will realize that negative comes with positive, right comes with wrong, good comes with bad, day comes with night. It's all about harmony. The nature of your mind is to have the balance and it does everything possible to create that.

7. **Its powerful beyond measures.**

It's said that no one could ever understand how powerful our mind is. Even legends like Einstein or Newton could not use more than 5% of their brain. Then how much do you think we are using! Yes this brain can make you achieve almost everything which you want. Its power still remains an immeasurable quantity. We compare one person with the other based on their achievements. For that's all that we have in our hand. So how do we measure the power of our own mind? By pushing our limits—taking that, so called, leap-of-faith, by taking positive risks, by trusting yourself and believing that you can do it.

The only thing which I can say at this time is that if you can tune your mind and energy with any task in this world then you will surely reach where you want to go.

Knowing all these laws of mind gets you to realise that

"If you really want to reach where you desire to reach then show your mind the right picture, visualize properly, don't push yourself rather be passionate about it and then you will see how things will change in your life with electric speed."—BSR

Thoughts become things—If you ask properly—and provided you know how to do so! Believe that you will achieve it—an absolute faith without any ifs and buts—then you will definitely get it—without fail—BSR

I made this sentence without a full stop in between because that's how it is supposed to go for the LAW OF ATTRACTION to be absolutely successful. As long as nothing comes in between, nothing will come in between your heart's desire and the realization of it.

A few days back I received a call from a lady. In her language she 'had to talk to me' after reading this book of mine and watching the video. She politely asked me if I had ample time because she wanted to narrate her story to me. And I was, of course interested. So here it goes—

She is from a small but very beautiful hill station called Shillong. Shillong is the capital of Meghalaya, and is situated in the north-eastern part of the country. It's one among the cluster of the seven states up there collectively called the seven sisters.

Shillong is also often referred to as the 'Scotland of the East', something she came to know at the tender age of twelve. She wanted to visit that place. She would spend hours on end searching for books and magazines to see pictures and read about Scotland. She was also surprised to notice that there was actually so much available about that faraway land and that too so easily. It also amused her around that time on, suddenly there was so much of talk about Scotland— either an article about it in the newspaper as a popular honeymoon destination or the sudden record snowfall this particular winter which has disrupted normal life. Then there was this story about the haunted dungeon right there in Scotland which is a part of history and an attractive tourist destination. A few days later her school friend for the last 7-8 years suddenly mentions about a cousin who is coming to Shillong on a family visit. Guess what? She is from Scotland! Then there is an announcement in the school of a farewell party for a particular young lady teacher. She was quitting her job because she was getting married ... and relocating to Scotland! "It was funny" she thought. "Why was Scotland all of a sudden crowding her from all different directions? A few days later she was subjected to an informal abrupt discussion between her brother-in-law and his friends about the difference in the English language spoken by the Scottish people and the rest of Britain! It was so much of it that she thought she was virtually transported there. But after sometime the regular life of a student caught on and Scotland was pushed to the background, though, even after so many years, she never forgot to add 'Scotland of the east' after Shillong, whenever someone asked her about her hometown.

Years later when she was of the marriageable age many marriage prospects were from Scotland. That rekindled her dream of visiting her dreamland but somehow none of them materialized. In-the-meantime she took up a job in Delhi and shifted her base there. There she met the man of her heart, once again pushed aside her Scotland dreams and got married to him. Even during the course of the marriage ceremony when someone commented "Hey, Shillong? Isn't it a hill station? I heard it's very beautiful", she would invariably swell with pride and say "Yes, it's very beautiful. It's also known as the Scotland of the East".

One week after marriage when her husband announced their honeymoon destination, she was reeling with excitement—yes, it was Scotland! An out of the world dream by an innocent school girl living in one remote corner of the world who knew no more about the place except that it was a part to learn in the map for her geography lesson . . . actually realised her dream.

She had dared to dream big, and innocent enough to spell out that dream to the universe and guess what, it was granted to her. Some super power in the universe said TATHASTU.

Not just that, her dream of buying a small red car with her own hard earned money when she grows up came true. And in her language, fell in love and got married to exactly the kind of person she had always dreamt about!

As a little girl she didn't have the knowledge of restraint. So she dreamt her wildest dream. And guess what? Her wildest dream was granted to her.

If you read her story carefully, you will realize that all the laws of mind were followed unknowingly by this lady. That's what happens with you. You already follow all the possible laws of the universe as there is no other way of living. The unfortunate thing is that you are not aware of those laws.

When I wanted to follow my heart and had a strong desire to make a difference in the lives of people, I didn't know how to do it. So I left my job and started my company called—*Challenging Horizons*. The real challenge came when I didn't have any experience of running companies or being an entrepreneur. I hired few people—however I didn't know how to utilize their maximum capacity. I had people, I knew they were capable of working but I couldn't keep them engaged. As a matter of fact they were directionless and a point came where either I had to ask them to leave or they themselves left.

I had people, I knew they could have delivered and as per my knowledge at that time I did my best with them but still I landed up in the situation which exhausted me. My ignorance was the reason for me being in this situation. Had I known how to really keep them engaged, I am sure the situation would have been different.

Most people don't know that they can really learn and remember at the speed of a computer. They still use their memory power to store the information the way they want. I was also one of them until I met someone who remembered 100 words in less than 5 minutes and with 100% accuracy. After 5 minutes he could tell me everything in reverse order and random order. I was surprised and asked a question—how can it be possible and a reply came—you can also learn it and that too in 3 days. I did the same and realized that now I can also do the same. I was unaware of my own memory power and was using it without awareness and the moment I became aware, I am using the same thing in a much better way. I can also teach you this art in just 24 hours. It's not rocket science, but it will give you the insight to what your mind can achieve if you put your heart into it.

In the same way you have unlimited power right this moment. Power in the form of your mind, the universal laws, if you get to know how to use them for your benefit you can always get better results. Most people use them but don't know how to use them in the right way to get maximum output. I am sure you would love to get the best in your life. So here I reveal some of the secrets for you to reach to your ultimate destination.

The Universe says your wish is my command. Every time you make a wish it just says Tathastu. Every time you feel a certain way it says—I will give more of the same to you. Every time you say something— that's what it takes as its command. It has no brain of its own. It just works and has no ability to identify what is good or bad and what is right or wrong.

There is a common saying that in life if we refuse to accept anything but the best, we usually get it. As the universe says—AND SO IT IS . . . .

So what is mind power, LAW OF ATTRACTION and universal power? How do they work? Are these just thoughts of motivation or is there anything substantial to talk about?

Listen to this, for I am sharing it with you—

This whole world is a magnet. Our Universe is a huge ball of energy. This is not something that I am claiming. It's pure science. If you open a book of physics from the 8th standard they will tell you that everything in the universe can be microscopically broken down into its element. Each element can be then broken down into molecules, which can further be broken down into atoms which have protons, neutrons and electrons in different combination that in turn marks the character of that element. Physics will tell you that all these protons, neutrons and electrons are never at rest. They are governed by the LAW OF ATTRACTION. Protons and electrons attract each other like magnetic poles because protons are positive and electrons are negative. Positive and negative poles attract each other. Neutrons are neutral. They are constantly vibrating within a set orbit with a certain defined energy. When this energy is challenged due to proximity to some other element with a stronger magnetic field that can change their combination, attract their protons, neutrons and electrons, they change form. They combine into something else.

Science will tell you that nothing in this world can be created or destroyed. They can only change form, but still exist. Always exist. Water, when subjected to heat becomes vapor, when frozen, becomes ice. All three of them have distinctly different characters but comes from the same elements—a combination of hydrogen and oxygen in different strength.

Everything works with one infinite power. Every bit in this universe, from a speck of dust to us humans, is a power house of energy. We are governed by one law—the LAW OF ATTRACTION. And we—humans are the most powerful magnet in the universe. And when we think, we emit unfathomable magnetic power to the universe. The stronger our thoughts the stronger are the signals that we are sending to the universe. If we are thinking about money we knowingly or unknowingly attract everything that has to do with money. If your thoughts are set at earning more money you will automatically attract avenues that will yield you money. On the other hand if that very thought of yours is clouded with fear—fear of losing money, being robbed, doubts in your own ability to earn it—that's exactly what will be happening to you. By thinking more money you will probably be attracting more money but your negative thoughts will also be attracting those negative vibes from that very universe resulting in probable money loss.

The universe obeys the LAW OF ATTRACTION as they receive these signals and combine them in the desired combination. No signals are lost. No thoughts, when thought with the complete power of the mind has ever been disobeyed. No wish has been left unfulfilled. No desire left incomplete.

The law of nature knows just one thing—"HOW TO GIVE YOU WHAT YOU ASKED FOR."

It does not operate with a logic or reasoning. It does not know how to differentiate between good or bad. It just says I give you everything which you want. If a person was to jump from the 5th floor and land on the ground without any cushioning—he/she will die, it does not matter if that person was good or bad. That is how the LAW OF ATTRACTION works. "YOU ASK IT DELIVERS".... the universal law that governs the entire universe.

You just need to be aware of it always, and consciously apply it to your everyday life. There is no limit to it. No ceiling applies in the LAW OF ATTRACTION. The universe has in abundance for every single person who believes he can. It does not apply a quota in its granary— there are SIMPLY NO LIMITATIONS. The only condition here is to make a wish, as big as you want, and believe in it with all your heart. Live it, breathe it, eat it and sleep with it. Definitely do sleep with it because even when we are asleep our subconscious mind are at work and keeps sending powerful signals to the universe. It's extremely important that we set free the greatest wish of our life and see the magic of our own mind come to play.

There are 3 major underlying beliefs which people operate from and they are the major reason for some people living their life with fulfilment and some people living it in an unsatisfied manner. These underlying beliefs are:

1. Belief that there is LACK of what they want.
2. Belief that there is ENOUGH of what they want
3. Belief that there is MORE THAN ENOUGH of what they want

Let me explain to you what they are and what role they play in someone's life

1. ***There is a Lack***—People with lack syndrome are people with Limiting thoughts. These people believe that there is a lack of everything. They are a miser even with their dreams. They like to restrict their dreams because somewhere during their growing up years they were taught to believe that dream is synonym to greed and greed is always bad. A greedy person is always a bad person and so on. There is also the belief that if you dream for too much it never gets fulfilled. The fear factor is always dominant and develops distrust about their ability. They don't believe that they can do it.

    Ask them "What about the other person right beside you who has done it?"

    "He is different. I am a simple man. I can't make a magical life story like him. Everyone is not lucky to have everything in life."

What is this thought process? This is nothing but an example of operating from the mind set of not having enough.

There are many people whom I meet and who tell me "I will be very happy when I achieve my goal". And when I ask them are you happy right now—they say "Not sure, but I am sure when I reach my destination I will be super happy". WOW! What an irony of the situation—how can you remain sad while creating your own life and designing your destiny?

Let me warn you:

If you remain sad or operate from there, it's just a message to the universe that you are operating from a belief which says—THERE IS A LACK IN MY LIFE. And if you have understood what I have said till now, then you also might have understood that the universe 'only' responds to your feelings and thoughts. You remain unhappy! Sad! And feel low! When you really doubt the universe and are not sure whether you will get them.

This very belief is a reason between those 80% people who keep struggling to turn their dreams into reality and those 20% who have been able to really live most of their dreams.

If you are to create magic in your life you will have to learn to get rid of these limiting thought processes and start by believing that there is enough in the universe for everyone. There is no lack there. Every 'lack' is in your mind. Every obstacle created by you.

An almost perfect example is a phase of my own life . . . .

Born in an ordinary family in a village called Khatoli, situated in Ajmer District of Rajasthan, life was very difficult. My father was a farmer and there was never enough. A sweetened, coloured ice block worth 50p sold by the sixty years old unkempt bleary eyed old man at the corner of the street, which we kids knew as ice-cream, was sheer luxury. We had to budget for that too! My father always tried to make allowance for our studies.

As I grew up, father managed to arrange money and I completed a course on computers from NIIT. I was good at it but there was a challenge. My spoken English was restricted to single words and phrases. A complete sentence was a mammoth task. When I had to deliver my first presentation at the institute, in English, I bolted up! I walked up on the stage but spoke nothing. I knew I had to do something about it. A few weeks later there was this get-together in the institute where everyone was asked some fun questions. When it was my turn, they asked me how I would convince my parents for marriage if I happen to fall in love with a lady 7 years older than me. The question was asked in English! And I did not really understand the meaning of the word 'convince'. There were five hundred people present in that auditorium! All I could say was 'I will elope'—and that too in Hindi. All 500 people laughed at me and amidst that laughter I heard a voice—"Please repeat the questions, in Hindi also for those people who don't understand English."

I was deeply embarrassed and it haunted me for many days. I tried learning English, but didn't really do me any good. What kept me going was that I did not want to become a farmer, work in the mills or supply raw materials to factories. I wasn't exactly sure what I wanted to do, but I wanted to do something different, something that I will enjoy doing. Exactly what, I didn't know—then. This thought pushed me to learn and I had started speaking some English and also secured myself a job in a call center only to be soon thrown out. The training team at that office said that my English was beyond repair. They said I was un-trainable!

One by one I worked for five companies. Something very strange about this period was that every company I had worked for, I was either thrown out or the company shut down. Guess it was a signal for me that I was meant to do something different. It took me a while longer to decode that signal from the Universe. By then I had repeatedly proved that I am a loser to myself and everyone around. I was jobless. Negativity had set in deep till I cut myself from the world around me. Every morning I would dress up and go out for interviews knowing, for sure that I will not be able to crack a single one. And predictably I came back home in the evening defeated. I know it probably sounds like a cheap plot right out of Bollywood movies of the yesteryears, but not when you are the protagonist and the cameras are missing!! There was nothing left in the world, at least not for me. I did not ask for much. I did not dream big. I just wanted to live with a little dignity and even that was denied.

Much later in my life, when I looked back and analysed, I realised that . . . I of course had a thought bank from which I was operating. I got to see everyone struggling since childhood. I got to see my parent's struggling, my friends struggling, relatives struggling, every villager doing hard work . . . . this cultivated the belief that life is hard and there is not enough for everyone. There is a lack. I also didn't know that I had this belief until I got to meet a few enlightened people and true masters who showed me the mirror and made me realize what I am capable of doing. The biggest realisation which I got was that I have everything which I want but I just need to learn how to train myself to use all those powers within. The student inside me got ready. One after the other I started meeting my masters who could train me and share their wisdom with me.

One of the most powerful masters whom I met during my journey is Shree Nithya Shanti who was a forest monk and now shares his teaching with many around the world. One day when I met him and shared with him that I feel low about myself, when I meet people who are more intelligent, more learned and are educated from the best of the schools in the world. I feel that I have no knowledge and don't know how I would achieve all those dreams which I really have been holding in my heart. Upon this Shree Nithya Shanti said—"Can you ever compare a tabla with a sitar? A Sitar with a guitar? A Guitar with a flute?" I said "No". Can a tomato be compared with a potato and a potato with radish? I again said no. He said "Bhupendra, we all are human beings but there is no way we all can be compared with each other. We all have a different role to play in this world. When we compare, we insult our own creator indirectly, as we blame him for making us the way we are".

He further stated—"We are great the way we are. We have almost all the possible knowledge which we want, the only thing we need to learn is to connect to our own Higher Self". I got confused and didn't understand what Nithya Shanti had just said. I asked him what does that mean. He said "Can you answer this questions of mine—how did Gautama Buddha, Bhagwan Mahaveer, Swami Vivekananda get their immense knowledge? Do you think they read all the books in the universe or they had Google as their support system?" I instantly said no. Nithya Shanti said "They got this knowledge by connecting to their inner self, by accessing their own powers of brain, by learning to believe in their own judgments and by having full faith in their creator".

The day I started following the path which my guru shared with me I started feeling great about myself and I started coming out of this belief that there is a lack, as previously, that was the only belief I was operating from.

"People with this kind of thought process really do not achieve much from the universe. They grow old and die trying to make some living with perhaps some perceived dignity."

2.   *There is enough*—While you aspire for more you simultaneously need to count your blessings—an attitude of gratitude. It's good to want a brand new car, but be thankful for the one you already have, if you aspire for a dream body be thankful for the one you are presently in, or if you are reeling in poverty be thankful that you are still alive and that there must be some purpose for it. There are some people who do go through certain lows in their life but they recover using this positive thinking. They make a quick calculation of what they have and use it as a trampoline to bounce back.

Few people operate out of this belief and guess what—they live a happy and blissful life.

Have you seen some people being less stressed than others? Have you seen people taking life as it comes? Those are the people who operate from this belief pattern and I am sure you will agree that this is a better belief system to live with in comparison to the previous one.

Continuing to give a real example out of another phase of my own life!.

I had by that time hit the rock bottom and instead of planning my next job interview, I found myself planning an escape—suicide. Yes you read it right—I was planning to end my life. I would explore painless options of dying. "Is jumping from the highest building comparatively less painful than drowning in water? Shall I slit my wrist?" I would think hard or "should I do an overdose of sleeping pills". I later zeroed down on lying down across a railway track and let the locomotive do the rest. With that thought predominantly on my mind, I headed towards the railway station when by chance I met a friend who, ignorant about the frame of my mind, forced me to accompany him to his friend's birthday party.

I went.

And the phase passed.

Later I realized that dying would do me no good, except hurting a few loved ones. I had no option but to make a U-turn or to bounce back. And that's exactly what I did—bit by painful bit. Till then I was concentrating on what I do not have—I do not have a proper education, I do not have money, I cannot speak English, I do not have a job, I do not have . . . I thought now that I have a no good list of do not's, why don't I make a list of the things I have?! To begin with, I have a life and a perfectly functional body and mind to go with it. Isn't that a good start? I have some education, some money and am young enough to make it all work.

Once I totalled that up, I realized that I felt good about myself—after a long, very long time. And I made this a practice. I started thinking that I have always got what I really wanted, to live my life and run with speed. This thought relieved me from all my tensions and worries. It felt so peaceful. It made me feel that I have blessings around me, that I am not alone. That my parents and friends love me and I can count on them. The truth is they were always there. Only I could not see them. I was so busy counting the curses. Slowly I started counting my blessings and it filled me with positive energy.

When I grew a little older and met my first guru he shared with me one of the secrets of winning in life. He said "Can you make a diary and write 10 daily achievements everyday". Upon this I replied "Sir I don't have 10 achievements in my life till today and you are asking me to write 10 every day!" He said "Yes, 10 everyday". And then he explained "Those achievements can even be very small in nature like you bringing smile on someone's face by appreciating them".

One very good thing which I like about myself and which I believe is the major reason of success for me till today is that whatever my trainer or guru says I follow it religiously. And that's what I did.

I started my little diary called **Victory Journal**. And started listing down 10 small victories every single day.

While writing this book I am re-reading a few which I wrote, when I first got introduced to this concept:

1. Hurray!—Today I reached office in time.
2. I have finished my assignment successfully and I am very happy about it.
3. It felt great to help my friend repair his bike.

The effort was little, but the effect profound. It loaded me with the feeling of goodness. I was happy.

By this time I had this burning desire to learn English. All my aspirations came to full stop there. I knew I had to, wanted to. I started again with a renewed sense of succeeding. Surprisingly I started liking myself too. When I stood in front of the mirror I saw someone handsome. It made me laugh happily!

I worked till I reached the first step to my destination.

I learned my English . . .

Good enough to address a thousand people attending my sessions,

Good enough to not need to revert to Hindi when talking to people, who spoke in English,

Good enough to forget that the language is not my mother tongue.

I was delighted. I had more things to be thankful about at the end of the day and more points to add each day in my victory journal. I didn't know that this mere act could have such huge effect. It was changing me bit by bit and I could feel the change vibrating within me with renewed force every single day.

During that course of time I got introduced to a concept called the **'Power of Purpose'**

It says that every person is born, for a purpose. God did not send us just to occupy space on the earth. And in order to live that purpose, he has also gifted you and me with something called . . .

Unique Ability:

Yes I can tell you with my experience that right this moment you have that one ability which is different than other. You can do at least one thing better than others; you have that special talent which can differentiate you from others. The earlier you discover it the better it is for you. That's what all the successful people did. They didn't go on learning new things. They did only one thing. They had a unique ability and they harnessed it. They worked on their strengths and that's what made them achieve the pinnacle of success . . . Yes you got me right—unique ability can't be created, it can only be discovered as it's the part of you and your whole system. Do something to find it and then work on it. It's only when we work on our unique ability we make ourselves happy. And when we happily indulge in something we automatically excel in that.

So, stop here and ask yourself your unique ability. Drop the book on your chest once again and jog your mind. What is your unique ability?

You don't know? Ok. Then ask yourself what is it that your heart desires most for that is your unique ability? What is it that's burning through your innards? Remember that whatever it is, it may not be acceptable to the world at large. People will sometimes oppose you, make you look like a fool, discourage you and coax you to give up. But this is your test. The universe tests your desire before granting it to you. It will also give you signals from time to time whether you are right or wrong. You need to decode them and march ahead. You need to trust the LAW OF ATTRACTION and know that whatever you desire the Universe conspires to give it to you.

When I wanted to speak about LAW OF ATTRACTION and share the secret of success to the world at large I again and again hit dead ends. Nothing worked for me and every day I was pushed back—or so I thought. I knew I could do it. But nothing happened. I kept a job to keep myself alive but that's not what I wanted to do, but how to drop this job which has been taking care of me since long. What will I do after that, how will I survive? Millions of questions raced through my mind and several were poised by others. I wanted to follow my heart, go with the flow but those questions put huge barriers around me.

I fought with myself and with the world around. I was tired of fighting and was about to give up. Then one fine day, as I was riding the bike, my thoughts clouded with doubts and I was ready to quit when I looked up at the sky and asked God his plans for me. I said "Please God, tell me if I am doing the right thing or not? Give me a signal. At least, something that will tell me that I am on the right track".

Immediately a miracle happened and my cell phone rang. The person on the other side said there is an opportunity to deliver a 3 days training program in WIPRO Pune and the next sentence was—"Bhupendra would you be interested in doing this". That was it. Eureka! I could decode this powerful signal from the universe and acted immediately by conveying my decision to my family and by resigning from my job. Yes, the Universe gives you signals at every step but only the ones who have burning desire in their heart and who are ready to learn can decode these signals. One of the arts which I would recommend you to master is to learn how to decode the signals of the universe, because the day you master this art, your life would be a lot easier and you will start growing faster. Trusting the universe is the only way of flowing smooth and rising with speed.

The second important thing which I would love to mention here is that Universe loves speed. If you don't act when you have the thought then this thought will vanish, the momentum will break. So . . . ACT . . . . and ACT now . . . When there is a thought and your heart is convinced about it then just take action. When you decode a signal don't wait for judging if it's right or wrong—whatever is the first voice in your heart just follow it . . . . GO WITH THE FLOW.

It was then, I have never looked back, never stopped and never gave up. Never asked how or why? I have learned that these are stupid questions. They waste time. All we need to do is have a burning desire and believe in it. That's it. That's all there is to it and the Universe provides.

So there is something I would want you to do. I would want you to follow what I call the "POWER OF 5". Yes! The power of 5 is extremely powerful in turning around your entire destiny.

What you need to do is this:

Make a journal and write the following things in it every single day without fail:

1. **5 Small or big victories of yours**

This I have already explained you and have shared in the example above. But the only thing I would like to mention here again is—don't forget to add at least one feeling word to it when you write. Like 'great' or 'wonderful'. This will help you align yourself, your right kind of desire and if you continue this practice for long you will see that your actions and thoughts will refine and start shining.

2. **5 Reasons of why you would love yourself more today**

One of the abilities of great masters is that they could understand the power of self-love. If you don't have reasons to love yourself then why would the world love you? Write it and then you will see the magic happening. The examples can be:

- I love myself as I helped a blind person.
- I love myself more as I saved a bucket of water.
- I love myself as I made someone happy today.
- I love myself as I wrote an article today.

3. **5 Desires of yours**

Write about those 5 desires which you really want to fulfill. They can be small or big. Don't worry about them at all. You just write your desires. Write them as if they are already fulfilled and you are enjoying the benefits of them. They can be wild or unrealistic desires but do write them. Few examples are

- I now have a wonderful limousine and I am traveling with my family in it.
- I am a very famous personality.

- I am the richest man in the world.
- Everyone who meets me falls in love with me.
- I can now fly high in the sky.

4. 5 blessing of the day

Counting your blessings is one of the most powerful ways to keep your feet grounded and spirits high. It helps you live in gratitude which is the feeling with highest frequency. When you count your blessings, you feel rich and live in abundance. When you operate out of abundance what will come into your life: nothing but abundance. Few examples:

- I am thankful as my friend carried my bag for 100 meters
- I am thankful as a shopkeeper dealt with me with happiness
- I am thankful as my client appreciated me for my new shirt
- I am thankful as I am able to afford a dinner in a five star hotel

5. 5 qualities which you want to have in you

Write about those qualities which you want to have in your life and again my instructions are—write as if you already have those qualities. Examples

- I am very honest and humble.
- I am a great leader.
- I take positive risks.
- I love others selflessly.
- I live up to my commitments.

- I am very energetic.
- I am very active.

Keep it to yourself and read it every day. Learn to say

THANK YOU . . .

More often and mean it each time you say it. Trust me; it will do more good to you than the person you are saying it to. When you are thankful for certain things in your life, you are attracting more of those things back to you. You are concentrating on good things and they expand. So let's say if you are thankful for the little money that you have, or the small house or the 1977 make car, you will be attracting more of everything to you—more money, a bigger house, a new car. That's a very simple theory of the LAW OF ATTRACTION.

3. ***THERE IS MORE THAN ENOUGH***—There are people who just can't get enough. They are always very excited and enthusiastic about everything around them. When they think, they don't put barriers in between their thoughts or a boundary wall to their dreams. For them the sky is the limit and everything in between is theirs to claim. They are a **no-limit personality or no-limit mentality** people. They believe that there is more than enough in the Universe and they just need to be there to receive it. They believe in receiving. While some people like to choose and chase they look at the universe as an ocean of possibility. For them it is unconceivable that they want something badly enough and will not receive it. They throw their net of desire mid-ocean with hope and faith and ask for everything their heart desire.

These people are usually great people with great names. They are great names today because they believed in the impossible. While we have names like Albert Einstein, Thomas Alva Edison, Mahatma Gandhi and Neil Armstrong of the yesteryears there are names like Laxmi Mittal the business magnet, Yuvraj Singh, Bill Gates, and Amitabh Bachchan of today to inspire us and to reaffirm that the universe has not stopped making people of that stature.

The Universe still says "I give you what you want" to everyone who follows the principle of the LAW OF ATTRACTION.

Yes there is always more than enough in this world but the irony of the situation is less than 1 % people live as per this belief and that's the reason only 1 % people hold the 99% percent wealth and rule on 99% population. Universe and nature don't know what lack means. Only the human mind has created this concept of lack and more.

People, who operate from this belief system, live in an ambience of possibilities not in a cloud of fear. They always think of receiving more as they don't doubt themselves and the universe. Doubting only comes when we operate from the belief "What if I don't get something". The fact is that universe will never say NO to you if you know how to ask it, believe it and receive it. If you know how to get tuned with the universe then harmonious music is the only possibility.

Negative thought have negative effects on us. This law, by science, is powerless on others. Because the thoughts are ours, the vibes or the signals that we are emitting belongs to us, which means we are connecting with them, so it comes back to us. You cannot wish something bad to happen to someone else and make it happen. Because YOU are thinking of that bad thing, that thing comes to YOU. The other person is probably not even aware of it. But if you are trying to attract someone to yourself that wish will be granted because you are thinking about that person and connecting signals back to you.

Why? Because everything that's coming into your life you are attracting into your life. And it's attracted to you by virtue of the images you are holding in your mind. It's what you are thinking. Whatever is going on in your mind you are attracting to you. Every thought of yours is a real thing—a force.

So once again I would want to remind you of the virtue of positive thinking! I know you must have heard it a million times, but now is when you get to understand its true meaning and its power!

All religions across the globe talk about it. You can pick up anyone of them and it's there. It's always been there for anyone to discover. It began at the beginning of time and will live till eternity . . .

Have you realized that places of worship have a unique sense of peace and serenity surrounding them? Even people who claim to be non-believers cannot deny the calming effect it has on their nerves. It is almost therapeutic. Taut nerves uncoil, the mind relaxes and the soul calms down. You will always find lots of people sitting in a temple or any place of worship. Talk to them and they will tell you that they come there for 'peace of mind'. How can a concrete structure that is then named a temple or a mosque or church or gurudwara give someone a sense of peace more than their home or any other beautiful place. I am sure there are so many other plush beautiful places in our neighbourhood. Then what gives?

I will tell you: The sense of unique peace and tranquillity comes from all the positive thoughts and goodness that circulates those places. No matter what the mental frame of a person is, he or she enters the house of God with goodness in their hearts. At that moment they try not to contemplate revenge or plan evil. They try and enter with a clean heart and pray for goodness. These positive thoughts of all the people together create positive vibes that zoom in and out and loop little circles of happiness around the devotees. That's why even a wasted dilapidated structure, hidden amidst the jungle which has God dwelling in it gives people that sense of tranquillity which the biggest, tallest mightiest building fail to deliver.

It is the law that determines the complete order of the universe, every moment of your life and every single thing you experience. It doesn't matter who you are and where you are. The LAW OF ATTRACTION persists and is forming your entire life experience and it's doing so through your thoughts! Right now! It is the greatest and the most infallible law upon which the entire system of creation depends.

There are some simple yet effective ways that comes under the heading—

1. Appreciate yourself and the world around
2. Live in gratitude
3. Feel good
4. Think big
5. Focus on what you want

Why do I call these simple? Because they are really very simple, as simple as it sounds. Even implementing them is simple. Yet what stops us from implementing them is pure laziness. I know after saying so much and laying down theories of success, the word 'Laziness' is a dampener. Some of you must be frowning at the choice of word and murmuring, "OH! But I am not lazy!" But when you have got all the tools you need to be successful, and yet if you are not, what's stopping you is your own mind. The various mind blocks, and sheer laziness. Identifying your laziness as laziness and acknowledging it is also very important so as to isolate it and eradicate it from your system. How to do it? We'll get to know in a short while.

By the end of this book you will successfully be able to hand pick and isolate all your strengths and weaknesses and use it to your advantage.

So read on . . .

Have you ever wondered why rich people are rich? Why does it seem to you that someone has everything and you have nothing? Or worst still, have you ever wondered why God the almighty has given someone everything and you nothing? How unfair he is, the One above! Why is it that everything goes wrong with you, and only you?

The 'poor me' syndrome who is bogged down by the hands of fate or destiny and seems to have nothing in his power?—

"My mother is terminally ill and my wife is going to have yet another baby and I have just lost my promotion that was due to me, and my car suddenly got some problem with the engine and that influential person who was supposed to help me is out of station and the weather too is not good and the food is rotten and I have a headache, back ache and I can't sleep . . ." . . . have you ever done that or have come across people who do that—share a cup of tea in an office break and he/she opens up a Pandora box of woes in their life? You must have sympathetically heard their stories and offered words of comfort, extended a hand of help. Well, next time don't! I am not asking you to be rude here. But be a true friend, by telling him that every bit of it is attracted to his life by his thoughts. Offer him help by asking him to choose his thoughts from now on and be positive about everything for the next 30 days, no matter what happens. And see the magic! And I do call it magic. So what if you cannot see the magician's wand waving mid-air or the hopeful colours of your thoughts that signals carry to the Universe? It's definitely there with all its magnanimous force and is acting out right now.

You can choose . . . Because science says so . . .

Reticular Activating System (RAS)

There is a portion of the brain which is called the **Reticular Activating System (RAS)** that allows you to choose.

RAS plays and important role in a person's ability to achieve his goals. Now what is RAS?

Let me tell you.

Imagine you are in a book fare. A heavily crowded ambience and you suddenly lose contact with your partner with whom you came to the fair. There are all kinds of ambience noise as befitting a fair. Noise of people talking to their friends, walking, music, microphone etc. Even though all the sounds come to you not all of them register. And then you suddenly hear your name or your friend's name being announced over the microphone. Suddenly your attention is full on. Your RAS is that automatic mechanism in your brain that brings relevant information to your attention immediately. RAS is like a filter between your conscious and sub-conscious mind. It takes instruction from your conscious mind and passes them on to the sub-conscious mind. May be it has instructions for picking your name when anyone calls it or that it is looking out for your friend's name.

Have you ever noticed that sometimes you are fast asleep amidst a room full of people, with the TV switched on and in full volume and some traffic noise filtering in from the window? But once you fall asleep nothing disturbs you except when someone calls your name. Then you find yourself responding even in your deep sleep which later you may not be aware of at all.

That's because the RAS responds to certain pre-set instructions and most people are tuned in to be alert to their names. So while the sub-conscious filters out all other noises, it **chooses** to pick out your name and act.

So why do I say **choose**? That's because we can deliberately program the RAS to choose the exact message from the conscious mind. Like setting a goal or saying affirmations or visualizing the goal.

Napoleon Hill once said that—

"We can achieve any realistic goal by thinking about it and stop thinking anything negative about it".

This means that if our thought says that we will 'NOT' achieve our goal, our Reticular system will see to it that we do NOT achieve it because 'NOT' here is the dominant thought.

So what we need to do is create a very definite picture of our goal in our conscious mind. It then passes over to the sub-conscious which then automatically attracts or brings to our attention all relevant information which otherwise would have been oblivious to us. It also filters out, somewhat, the unnecessary.

So if you want to create your own destiny and reality, get your Reticular Activating System to work. Why that is important is because the RAS is deciding what you're putting your attention toward.

If you want to know more about RAS then I would like you to follow the below link of the PDF which is written by Montana Gray. This will help you find some powerful exercises as well about how to program the RAS and create the results which you want.

http://www.angelavatar.com/ras.pdf

The LAW OF ATTRACTION says 'like attracts like'. So as you think a thought, you are also attracting like thoughts to you. If you are thinking of more money, it's more money that you will be attracting, sometimes mysteriously. Like a cheque from a saving policy that has just matured or some forgotten Aunt who has written wealth for you in her will! If you are worrying about losing that money constantly, you will find an invisible sucking machine at work that is sucking out your earned money. If you are thinking of illness, you will never ever be always fit. If nothing else, you will always find yourself bogged down with a persistent headache. If you are thinking of love, it's love you will get. If your thoughts say "I love that person so much but that person doesn't love me at all", no matter how hard you try, you will never get that desired love from that person. If you fear that the only 3 topics you did not revise for your exam out of the 20, will appear in your question paper, guess what, they will definitely come. If you fear that when on a long drive your car will breakdown in the middle of nowhere, it will surely do. Whatever your predominant thoughts are it will materialize.

If you recall the story of Aladdin and his magic lamp, there is a genie that pops out of the magic lamp when rubbed and says "Your wish is my command!"

The magic lamp is your mind, the genies are your innumerable wishes, and as you activate those wishes every time by rubbing them with your thought process they materialize. And that's what it is—"Your wish is my command!" That's what the power of your mind is. Every time you make a wish, the genie says "Your wish is my command!" This demonstrates how your whole life and everything has been created by you. The genie will answer your every command with the assumption that that's what you want. Because be it positive or negative, that's what is dominating your thoughts—good or bad.

"If you can see it in your mind . . . you are going to hold it in your hands soon."

If that particular red car is something you have dreamt about even as you struggled to hang on the rails of an over loaded public transport and barely managed to pay for your dinner you are going to have it. The only condition is you need to make a commitment to yourself about having it and believe in it.

This is **VISUALIZATION**.

A very necessary step that fast tracks you towards the realization of your dream.

Believe that you have it, feel its touch, and imagine turning the car's key to open the door to the driver's seat. Feel the touch of black leather of the steering wheel in your grip, hear the car roar to life everyday as you turn on the ignition, see it roll out of the parking lot and zoom into the streets. Do it every day and it won't be long before that car stands in front of your doorsteps. If you don't believe me try it. It's the LAW OF ATTRACTION. It never fails!

Thoughts are magnetic and have a frequency that magnetically attracts all like thoughts of the same frequency. Everything sent out returns to the source, and the source is you!

While watching television, when we jog through channels with the press of a button on the remote, what exactly are we doing? We are changing the frequency. Every channel is broadcasted from the television station's transmission tower via a frequency and we need to match the frequency with the television set in our house in order to view it. When we want to see some different pictures on our television, we change the channel and tune in to a new frequency.

We are a human transmission tower, and we are more powerful than any television tower created by any human. Because we are a creation of the universe, the frequency we transmit reaches beyond cities, countries and beyond the world. It reverberates throughout the entire Universe. And we are transmitting that frequency with our thoughts!

So the pictures you receive from the transmission of your thoughts are the pictures of your life! Your thoughts create the frequency, attract like things on that frequency and broadcast it back to you as your life's picture.

If you want to change anything in your life, first change the channel and change the frequency by changing your thoughts.

"The world we have created is the product of our thoughts. It cannot be changed without changing our thinking."—Albert Einstein

But this 'changing of thoughts' or the 'thought process' is easier said than done. If you consciously monitor your thoughts for one single day, just one single day, you will realize that there is a definite pattern to it.

Research says that people think around 60,000 thoughts per day! Yes, that's true—sixty thousand. So these thoughts have a definite pattern, depending on various factors.

These factors can be broadly divided into two categories—

Positive thoughts and negative thoughts

It is seen that there are people who no matter what always indulge in negative thoughts. If something good happens to them they think it's now the turn for something bad to show up. They forget to be happy. They send all negative signals to the Universe, and keep sending them till something really ugly shows up and then they wisely claim "See I knew it was coming. For every single laugh, we are made to cry ten times over." They wake up in the morning and say "Cheez! I am late again". They then go to the bathroom and crib about the wet towel, the watery floor, then the tea is lukewarm, the breakfast not filling, the traffic too heavy, and the weather too hot . . . everything is negative. They crib and complain throughout the day till they go to bed at night. When they try to be positive they just land up justifying themselves. You will notice that these people never see the light of happiness till the end of their lives. Theirs is always a 'sad story of my life' to narrate. When you ask them during the passing—"Hey! How are you?" their response will never be the regular 'I am fine, how are you?' They will instead perhaps hand you over a detailed medical report with a plethora of complicated medical history.

On the other hand there are people whom I call bouncers. They seem to carry a trampoline around with them. No matter what the situation is they somehow manage to bounce back. Even when something bad happens to them they treat it as a 'time being situation' and know for sure that it's definitely going to change for the better.

We think that these people are always happy because nothing bad ever happens to them. We don't realize that nothing bad ever happens to them because they don't let bad things hover around them like a stinking halo for too long. They over power bad occurrence with positive thoughts. They push through mishaps with immense positive energy and believe in themselves. And once the strong signals are sent to the universe the entire universe conspires to say AMEN.

This is one story I heard it from my mother. Read this for every bit of it is true—

My mother was then unmarried and of the age when she went to college. Right behind her parental house was a rocky hill which was habited. People like house maids, cooks, carpenters among others built little huts and stayed there. They found work amidst their rich neighbours at the foothills. One fine rainy season the earth went loose and huge boulders tumbled from the hill top on to the huts below. It was bad. Two people had died in the incident, my mother recalls. Among them there were two families who were neighbours. Both had the same family structure—husband, wife, a son and a daughter—of the same age group. All the kids went to the same school in their locality. Both of them had a local shop each at the end of the lane on the foothills. They sold odd things, like groceries, stationeries, some medicines etc. The turnover was such that they barely sustained.

In the mishap both their houses were completely destroyed. Even pots and pans were not spared. My mother says that while one family wailed and cried incessantly, the other one sulked for some time but soon bounced back by counting his blessings—"My family is all safe," he would say, and "nothing happened to my shop so I am grateful to God for his mercy. While the other fretted over his massive loss, his neighbour started building from the pieces left.

His wife took up sewing and cleaning and he ran the shop. He did not let his kids miss their school for a single day and they appeared for their school finals that were just round the corner.

On the other hand, his sulking neighbour could not manage to reopen his shop for months on end, and went to his rich neighbours at the foothills for monetary help. While everyone understood in the beginning, they soon wore out. Their kids dropped out of school for good, while the other two kids did well in their studies. The neighbours, when they saw that they were trying hard, chipped in from time to time. Local boys club took in the responsibility of their school books, uniforms and stationeries and the school made exceptions for a needy pair of brilliant students and pardoned their school fees. Families donated clothes and utensils once in a while. They were always thankful for whatever they got, while it was tricky to extend a helping hand to the other family because they were never happy with things that were given to them and always wanted something more or something else.

Why do I narrate this story now? Because last time I went home, my mother informed me that the family who never stopped believing has received their dues from the universe. Their daughter was getting married to a pilot, her brother's friend, who too is a pilot. She herself is a school teacher and teaches in one of the 'A' grade English school of the city. We were invited to grace the marriage ceremony. My mother says that when the father came in with the invitation card, she asked if he was finally happy, now that his children are doing well in life. He replied that he was never unhappy. Infact he made sure that he was always happy with whatever he had in his life. "That's what sustained me and my family so long."

"What happened to his friend and their children?" I asked my mother.

"Their father is bedridden due to Lung cancer. And their mother too is always ailing, probably from prolonged poverty and hunger. The son tries to run the shop somehow, but now that there are better and bigger shops just round the corner, nobody visits their shop. The daughter takes care of the household work. I don't think she will ever get married. We all tried to help in the beginning, but he refuses to pull himself out. Slowly we all gave up."

She also said something in the run, because she doesn't know the LAW OF ATTRACTION. She said they can't blame them totally for their misfortune. "Somehow it seems even destiny betrayed them." She said. "While things happened for his neighbour just out of the blue, God, it seems, never looked at them. From nowhere their father, who was the only earning member, fell sick with a terrible disease. Their mother too could not go out to work because since the mishap, she was always ailing. One after the other bad things happened to them and they could never recover."

Does that ring a bell? For me it does, if I interpret the narration applying the LAW OF ATTRACTION. While one of them kept his faith and his thought process aligned with the universe for good things, the other magnified his misfortune, concentrated on his loss and tuned his thoughts to all the negative vibes of the universe.

The 'LAW OF ATTRACTION' said TATHASTU to both of them!

So, you need to **monitor your thoughts** and recognize your pattern. If you are someone who is more often happy than sad throughout the day, then you are in line with the positive energy of the universe. If you are grateful for all things big and small, if you know how to keep your faith and never lose hope, then no matter what rotten time you are presently thrown into, good things are just round the corner.

Having said that, it will be really difficult to monitor all sixty thousand thoughts one by one and analyse them. So how do you do them? Well, there is a trick. Stop! Now! And ask yourself how are you feeling? Are you happy at this moment or are you sad. Because you cannot be happy and have negative thoughts simultaneously or for that matter feel sad and think positive. It's just not possible. So every time you do a mood check you come face to face with your signal colour that you are emitting.

Please understand this, for this is a complete science, that there is no way you can attract good in your life with negative thoughts or do bad to yourself with lots of positive thoughts. Close the book around your finger for a couple of minutes and think. Think about all the bad things that have ever happened to you and even the good ones. Did you ever say this to yourself, in the past, that you had a 'hunch' that something is about to go wrong and it went wrong? Did you ever say things in your life like "Cheez! I knew this would happen!" or "I know it was coming!"? Dear friend, you were calling it, with lots of energy, into your life! You were asking for it. Even begging for it persistently till YOU made it happen.

You need to make it a practice—to stop every now and then, abruptly, and do a **'mood check'**. This will tell you about your flow of thoughts. If you find yourself depressed, or sad, or frustrated then your signals are negative. If you are upbeat, happy, energetic, then your signals are positive. Be sure something good is going to happen. Probably that pretty girl or that handsome guy you saw sipping coffee in the office canteen yesterday will walk up to you and say 'HI!' Just a thought, really!

How to Convert Negative Beliefs into Positives

If you are holding on to certain negative thoughts for longer time then there is a risk that you are giving birth to a negative belief. Yes—that's how the limiting beliefs or the negative beliefs are formed. Many people in spite of having all the things which it takes to grow are not able to grow because they have been a master in giving birth to these monsters called negative beliefs. These beliefs are so harmful that they kill all your creative muscles and block all the ways which lead you to freedom and abundance. These beliefs just make you weak and rob your powers from you.

Having done a mood check, for a definite period of time, if you find that your mood is consistently negative; try laundering it. Break these negative beliefs as soon as possible.

How do you break **NEGATIVE BELIEFS?**

It's a 6 step small process.

1. Identify that it's a negative belief
2. Stop reinforcing it with immediate effect

3. Understand that beliefs are not facts
4. Doubt & Challenge the negative belief
5. Think about the empowering belief with which you would like to replace this negative belief
6. Condition your mind with the empowering belief

But before jumping into the breaking of negative beliefs let's start with what are beliefs and how they are formed.

"Once there lived a wise old monk. Around him there were many other monks who were learning divine practices from him every day. So they all lived together. This wise old monk had a pet cat which he loved. They would all sit together and meditate. Every time they meditated together, this wise monk would tie his cat near him so it doesn't run around and disturb the others. This entire process continued for close to 30 years and one fine day this old monk passed away.

Now there was another senior monk who was taking lead in this entire process. For some reason they adhered to their 30 years habit of first tying the cat and then starting the meditation. The day they didn't find the cat they were sceptical. Their meditation felt incomplete. Finding the cat every day and tying it became more important than the meditation itself! They thought that the wise old man used to tie the cat because there was some logic and reason behind it. Not having the cat tied was perceived as breach of rituals. It felt ominous!

All the other monks developed the belief that it is a must to tie the cat if you are offering group meditation. They developed the belief that this mediation will not be successful if the cat is not tied".

What went wrong in this entire story? Someone did something for his own convenience and other people followed blindfolded. That's how the beliefs are formed.

If you hold a thought and you have enough experience to validate that thought then that becomes the belief. For an example: if you think you are wise and people come to you and appreciate you for your wisdom then with time you develop the belief that you are indeed very wise. The longer you experience the same, the stronger this belief becomes. It's easier to develop beliefs.

Such beliefs fall under two categories—the ones which motivates us and the ones which demotivate us. The beliefs which motivate us are called empowering or positive beliefs and the one which drains our energy are called as limiting or negative beliefs.

1. First you need to learn how to identify your negative beliefs. To identify the negative belief you need to first recognize those negative thoughts which are strong in your head and then validate them by asking few questions. For an example:

    Example no 1: I am not good with studies

    *   Is this a repeating thought?
    *   Does it make you feel bad?
    *   Is it stopping you from taking some actions towards your goal?
    *   How else does it stop your growth?

    These are negative beliefs, if it creates negative impact in your life. So, repeating thoughts which makes you feel bad and put restrictions on you can be a negative belief.

2. **Stop 'reinforcing' it with immediate effect:**

Without noticing, people keep reinforcing their negative beliefs by

i) Collecting false evidence that supports it

ii) Thinking about it over and over.

Both actions reinforce the negative belief and make it stronger. The first step to change a negative belief is to stop reinforcing it. You need to start by adjusting your perception of events and by not thinking about it over and over.

3. Understand the difference between facts and beliefs.

The best thing which I can tell you about your beliefs is that they are not facts. There is a huge difference between them. Facts never change but beliefs do. Facts are same for everyone but beliefs are different for different people. Fact is Shah Rukh Khan is a huge celebrity. Belief is that no one can be greater than him.

Hence don't think that your beliefs are the only way of living. Your beliefs are just one paradigm. Shift your paradigm and you will see how beautiful the world is.

4. Doubt & Challenge the negative belief
One of the best ways to change a negative belief is to challenge it and doubt it.

Some people come to my workshop and tell me that "I am not confident". I ask them what makes them believe that they are not confident. Upon which they share many incidents where they have proved their lack of it. I ask them the following questions to challenge their own negative beliefs:

• How do you know that you are not confident?
• Are you sure that you are not confident?

- Have you never been confident in your life?
- Don't you remember even a single situation in your life when you were confident?
- Can you doubt this belief of yours?
- Would you still lack confidence if your or your family member's life depended on you doing the right things?

Once I was addressing a group of 1000 + students and I realized that a large number of them were sitting together but not participating. This was bringing the energy level of the room down and of course it was not to my liking. I asked few of them to come on the stage for an activity. No one bothered to come. I invited repeatedly but still no one came up.

I got down from the stage and walked among the audience and asked a few to volunteer for the activities. They refused. I got a chair and sat in front of one student. My mike was on so everyone could listen to what we were talking about. I asked him why you don't want to come on the stage. He said "I have never been on the stage and that's why I am scared". I said "So how would the fear go away? Can it go away by just sitting in the corner in a chair?" He said "No".

I asked him "Do you want to be successful or want to remain ordinary?" He said "I want to be very successful". The next question was "Will you ever be successful by being fearful?" He replied "No". "How long do you think you want to live the same life which is full of fear?" "Not even a single more minute" was the reply. "So why don't you come and face this fear from the stage?" He said "No, I won't come. I am afraid". Upon this I gave him the following hypothetical situation:

"If you reach home today evening and find your mom on deathbed and her last wish is to see you speaking from the stage, speaking in front of 1000 people and they giving you a standing round of applause. Would you not fulfil that wish?"

"I will for sure" he replied. It gave me a chance to ask my next set of questions to him—"How do you know that your mom is going to be alive forever? Do you know how many people are losing their parents right this moment when we are talking?"

"I got up and walked up to the stage after asking these questions and guess what—the guy followed me to the stage. Even all those people who refused to be a volunteer also came on the stage and spoke from that platform".

Hence, can you challenge your negative beliefs? Can you ask yourself some powerful questions to shake your own thoughts and bring the best out of yourself?

5. Think about the empowering belief which would replace this negative belief.

Can you now start saying that I am the most confident guy in the world? Can you start saying this with lot of confidence and emotion? If yes then you are able to turn the negative belief into a positive one. Similarly, turn all your negative beliefs into positive ones, one by one. Follow step six if you have done this.

6. Condition your mind with the empowering belief:

Now is the time when the actual mind programming with the new empowering belief is done. How this programming needs to be done is as follows:

- Repeat the empowering belief as many times as possible. This is called affirmations.
- Catch yourself in all those times when you are living this positive belief. This will create a referral point in your mind. Create many such referral points to strengthen the belief.
- Model people are those who are already following this empowering belief. Try to imitate them and live the way they live. Try to map their thoughts and beliefs. Match their actions and talks. This will speed up the entire process.
- Change something in the outer world as soon as possible. This means you start doing things which doesn't remind you about your negative belief and remind you more about the positive belief.

It's criminal to have negative beliefs. If you are holding on to many negative beliefs then you are murdering your true self. You are putting yourself in an invisible cage which will never allow you to remain free. You are under-valuing yourself and limiting your own powers.

What are you waiting for—find out each negative belief and shatter them up right this moment. Yes I mean it. Right this moment! Close the book and practice it with at least one negative belief of yours.

Formula of Successful Manifestation

Have you noticed that people who are in love rarely have a sad story to narrate? It seems everything around them is just in sync. When they talk to their friends you will never catch them saying how utterly frustrating their bosses are or how much the knee is hurting. New lovers are almost never ill and all of a sudden they find themselves attracting lots of new things. Some new friends surely add up, the work place is more welcoming, they find a new job, or their business suddenly blooms. We call it the lady luck. Of all the signals known to mankind, love is the strongest. When you are in love, you emit such strong signals that everything gets attracted to you with the speed of lightening. Now can we comprehend the reason behind the age old saying,

> *'Love makes the world go round?!' Well, you never thought it was so literal, right?*

When I say love I just don't mean the Adam-Eve love. I mean love for everything. Even that small little red car which you pined for is love. Or that dream project for which you planned since you were a young kid or a visit to Scotland even when you were not sure if it was an amusement park some 30kms away or the name of the nearest pastry parlour! You loved it, with all your being and got it, in your hand.

By now you must be bubbling with excitement, wanting to know the hows? Please forgive me my grammatical liberty that I have exercised and go ahead and ask the question—"How do we do it? How do we make things happen? I work so hard and I am ready to do whatever it takes, but nothing seems to get me my heart's desire."

That's because there is a process to be followed. Some knowledge to be gained and skill to be practiced. I love the word 'awareness' too and hence you will find this word pop up again and again in the course of this book.

So now let's make ourselves aware of a few more things and find out how and why the LAW OF ATTRACTION works. We can then apply it in our lives. Daily lives. Yes, daily lives. And why do I specify that? Because the energy that circulates which enables the LAW OF ATTRACTION to operate is a never ending process. Energy does not stop. There is no vacuum. And no data is lost. Whether we acknowledge it or not, whether we are aware of it or not, energy is the atmosphere surrounding us. And we are constantly connecting with the LAW OF ATTRACTION via this very energy. So it will be a very good idea to know how to use it to our advantage in our daily lives.

There aren't any shortcuts. But yes, skills are involved and lots of awareness. Awareness of our own selves—our body, mind and soul. A logical, scientific connection between the heart and the mind that finally triggers happiness, fulfilment and satiation. The art of balance between them, that creates the magic.

There are four things I will be talking about that can have a profound effect on your life

1) *BURNING DESIRE*
2) *ABSOLUTE CLARITY*
3) *CONVICTION*
4) *HOPE & FAITH*

1. BURNING DESIRE

The LAW OF ATTRACTION says there is nothing in this world for which if you have a burning desire you do not achieve it. It does not happen. Never happens. The LAW OF ATTRACTION cannot contradict itself.

The first thing we need to do is ask—from whom? From the universe. There has to be a burning desire for that object for that's when your signals are the strongest. And only the universe can fulfil it for you. How? By following the link of the LAW OF ATTRACTION. Once you make a wish Affirm it over and over again to the universe. Don't make a wish and forget about it. The universe needs to be constantly in touch. Affirm your wish with words. Say it, repeat it, and write it down on the walls, paste stickers on the refrigerator door. When you want something badly enough, be loud and clear about it. Work your imagination to the smallest detail. Have a 3D picture of your desire in your mind and if possible on the walls.

Affirmation is the first step and the most important step towards realizing your burning desire.

And now that you know it's not your immediate neighbour but the Universe who is waiting for you to ask, all you need to do is express your wildest dream; and affirm it with all the strength of your thoughts. Focus on that thought and thought alone. Don't wait to analyse the sanity of your wish. Don't try to be considerate and dilute it. Don't minimize it or settle for something lesser. It will be foolish to do so when the Universe is there to grant it.

Think about this scenario. Hypothetical, of-course. But think when Neil Armstrong might have walked up to his mother with baby steps, sucking at his thumb and said he wants to walk the moon, don't you think his mother picked up her baby, kissed him hard and laughed at his baby wishes? But as he grew to an adult and still wished to travel to the moon, his mother must have swooned at his son's unusual psychological bent of the mind. But today we all know who that man is. Don't you think his dream was a little eerie? Well, not anymore. So just do this much for yourself—be fearless and ask whatever desire is burning in your heart.

But remember that this universe is very intelligent. It doesn't just believe in what you think your burning desire is. The moment you claim that you have a burning desire, this universe will put you through a series of tests. The one who clears all these tests is the one who conquers it all.

Here I want to grab an opportunity to share a small piece of my life. When I attended many self-help programs I got to see a 360 degree change in my life. I got to see that all my weaknesses were turning into my strengths one by one. I got inspired by all my teachers and the desire to become a breakthrough expert, a coach and a life transformer started taking shape in my mind. Every time I attended the sessions, the feeling strengthened. I immediately wanted to take a different route. All of a sudden my IT job stopped exciting me and my thoughts were focussed towards being the magic in transforming human lives. I was burning with this particular desire to become a Change catalyst.

Now was the testing time. This Universe started putting me through series of tests which I passed with flying colours and today living a life of bliss.

The major test I went through was to convince my parents and my friends and leaving my job to follow my heart completely. There were many practical challenges like: my job was really good, and I was earning a handsome salary. So justifying quitting this job was a challenge. And then should I quit, there was no financial support from any other place. Didn't know how I will survive once the steady flow of income stopped and how long will it take for me to start earning again in my new field of interest. Was not even sure who will come and sit in my program as I was new to the profession, there were many big names then and very few people knew me in the city.

It was a scary test as my entire life depended on it but I was determined. I started thinking about the worst case scenarios. I got to realize that the worst which can happen is that I might lose few lakh rupees and I might need to return to my IT job after 2-3 years. "Just that?" I thought, "Then I was up for it."

Luckily I had 1 lakh rupees cash stashed away and I thought this should be enough for me to survive for the next 1 year.

After a yearlong brainstorming I finally took a leap—a leap of faith. I could listen to the voice of my heart and jumped into this unknown field.

Parents didn't understand why I wanted to change my profession and jump into unknown territory. I faced strong resistance, but when the desire is fuelled by passion you always believe in yourself and follow through. I took my decision and moved ahead. Yes my family members got hurt initially with this decision and conveyed their unhappiness. But I was glad that I could clear this test.

There were times when my belief about my own abilities was shaken. I would be scared. One sentence gave me the power at that moment. And that was:

"It's not that winners are not scared. Winners win because they take actions in spite of the fear". It made me strong and helped me take action even when I was scared.

This decision of mine affirmed universe that yes I really had a burning desire in my heart, the desire to make a huge difference in the world around.

It's said that—if you really want something with all your heart than the entire universe conspires to give it to you. That's what started happening ever since I took this BIG, BOLD and BRILLIANT STEP. Yes I call it brilliant step because if I would be my previous self then I would never be able to take this step and would still be suffering doing a job I did not like and would have no freedom of operating from my own heart.

If you search deep within, you will realize that it is fear and fear alone of so many things known-unknown that stops us from dreaming and turning those dreams into burning desires. Like a person who earns just 7-10K per annum will be petrified of dreaming about owning a Jaguar car. They will not even allow themselves to dream about it. "What's the point? I will only make myself miserable. I will never be able to own it. Not even with my entire life's earning"—Will be his approach towards a mere dream. Forget about wanting to achieve it, he will be terrified even to dream about it or admire it!

"Question yourself this—what is that one thing you would have wanted to do if 'fear' did not exist".

For fear is just another hurdle of the mind, deep seeded in the conscious and the sub-conscious due to some past experience or acquired knowledge. Most of us are terrified of cockroaches even though it doesn't bite nor is it poisonous. This is fear. This fear will hold you back. Of all the fears known to mankind, fear of failure is numero uno. No matter what you set out to achieve, fear of failure comes first to your mind, even before the joy of a possible success, and makes the journey an uphill task, for you are constantly fighting the unseen. While the fear of failure is natural, it is important to remember that we should not let the fear of a possible failure over-power the joy of possible success. It's foolish, time consuming and absolutely useless. To make your mind focus affirmation is vital. The more you affirm to the universe with full faith and conviction you systematically obliterate the fear of failure, for two contradicting emotions on the same subject cannot stay together or hold the same strength. One has to die to let the other live. Methodical affirmation makes sure that your dream survives and thought of NOT achieving it fades away.

2. ABSOLUTE CLARITY

This is my favourite topic as many a times when I ask people what their goal in life is—most of them say they want more money. So I take out a 1000 Rupees note from my pocket and share it with them and say, "Look now your goal is accomplished. You now have more money than what you had a minute ago". The person immediately says—no, I want more means a lot of money. I just ask him a lot of money means how much? And then they have no answer as they have never decided how much. Similar way many people say—my goal is to be peaceful, I want to be happier in life. I just ask them how you would measure happiness and peace. How would the lord, the universe know that now you are happy and now you are more peaceful. And why should he serve you when everyone is asking him the same questions.

Clarity is the power. If there is no clarity then there is no manifestation.

There should be no ambiguity and no hiccups. You should be absolutely clear about what you want. Like at this moment I want to finish writing this book and get it published. And when I say this, the link of feelings, actions, words, emotions and thoughts should not be broken. One broken link will mean doubting your own self and will weaken the signals. You will be sending mixed colour signals to the universe. There will be strands of black mixed with the bold blood red of positive intent. The LAW OF ATTRACTION will not have the desired degree of manifestation. Depending on how much black is there in the red it will vary anything from delay to denial. Your signal of mixed colours is confusing the LAW OF ATTRACTION.

The LAW OF ATTRACTION works every time. It never fails. Like the law of gravity, LAW OF ATTRACTION too is universal and always in force.

Have you ever tried playing this game? If not, try it out, and observe it very carefully. I played it when I was a school going kid. I learned it as a part of my physics experimentation—The LAW OF ATTRACTION with respect to magnets. Take a piece of a bar magnet. It's easily available in all stationary shops. It will be a small iron bar of about 5cm long and one end painted red. That is to indicate the positive pole. The other side is automatically the negative pole. Pick up some small iron chips too. Now place a pinch of those iron chips on a piece of paper and run the magnet from under the paper. You will observe that all the iron chips quickly gather to accumulate in one place right above the magnet. If you flip the magnet to the other end the iron chips will scatter and gather again. We know that the positive ends of the iron gets attracted to the negative pole of the magnet and vice-versa. If you now take the positive end of the magnet and slowly run under the paper in one direction, you will observe that the iron chips arrange themselves beautifully and strictly in order with all the positive poles at one end and the negative poles at the other. Now try flipping the magnetic bar, alternating it's positive and negative poles. What happens? The iron chips dances merrily on the piece of paper forgetting the rules that binds them. You have confused them.

If you keep sending such mixed signals to the Universe, that's exactly what happens. You make them dance directionless. At the end you see no results, minimum results or even negative results. That's when you say "See, I knew it would not work. I always knew it wouldn't." what you don't realize is that this very doubt of yours has manifested itself. Obeying the LAW OF ATTRACTION it said I will give you what you ask for.

3. CONVICTION.

We surely need lot of conviction In other words believe in yourself.

"What you think about, you bring about."

A shortcut to the manifestation of your desire is that you see what you want to become as an absolute fact. People here apply to two categories of thought:

1. HAVE—DO—BE
2. BE—DO—HAVE—

The **HAVE-DO-BE** people are the ones we call the ordinary people. These people need to HAVE everything in order to DO something before they can become what they want to BE.

For an example, the person who is aspiring to have a physique like Salman Khan will first run to the sports shop and buy all the necessary sports gear. Then enrol in the gym. Then will have to take time out from his work and daily routine to wake up every morning to visit the gym. Will need to have a by-the-book proper diet and sleep well in order to do the needful and then become like Salman Khan. Anything missing in this order will be perceived as a huge hurdle and thus will prevent him from achieving his goal. That means if he, suppose, does not get the desired sports garments and shoes or that the gym is too far away from his house, or it is not adequately equipped. If his work hours are stretched and he can't get up early in the morning or that these days it's raining too heavily during those hours. It may also be possible that he is aspiring to follow a particular diet chart but is not being able to manage it on his own. All these will be huge blocks in the way of his success and he will fail every time. And he will successfully find someone else or something else to attribute his failure to. What he fails to understand is that one cannot control or dictate external factors. They are not responsible for your success. What is responsible for your success or failure is within you.

The other category is the **BE-DO-HAVE** people. They too were once ordinary people who made themselves extra-ordinary by turning the table. These people, if they want to become like Salman Khan they think themselves as Salman Khan from day one. They visualize that physique like Salman khan. They also visualize the benefits of that amazing physique; they hear those compliments well in advance and can feel the benefits in the present. As a result the doing part becomes autopilot for them. They don't have to push themselves for any physical activity. They go to the gym if possible, if not, they run in their backyards, they run along the railway line, they lift boulders and sand sacks to build their muscles and join chairs to do push-up. They hang on anything they can hang on to and do their pull-ups. They make themselves conscious of their diet not hyper and lose focus. Finally in a weird, reverse, way they become what they want to be—A Salman Khan.

These categories of people do not wait for opportunities to knock their doors or good times to come their way or the tides to turn in their favour. These people turn the wheel and make things happen. Everything else falls in place.

Let me ask you this—have you not followed the BE-DO-HAVE pattern ever. I am sure you have. In fact you followed it every single day when you were a kid. You wanted to play and really wanted to become the best in that way: did you ever have to think oh!—playing, means too much of running, too much of energy wasted and on top of that, it will take too much of time. Unknowingly you wanted to have lot of fun. You felt that and action part of it was autopilot and you didn't have to do much for this. You played, played hard, got exhausted but still wanted to keep playing. Ultimately you got what you wanted and that was a lot of happiness, satisfaction, peace. In short as a child you lived every single day the BE-DO HAVE fashion. This is the real secret of success which every great sportsman, businessman, body builder and film maker follows. In fact all those people who are in the top 1% bracket live this philosophy.

HAVE-DO-BE and **BE-DO-HAVE** is a very powerful concept. You need to recognize your pattern—no cheating please!—And turn it around to your advantage. It's really very easy, once you correctly analyse and acknowledge your category and help yourself.

This thought process of 'BECOMING' what you want to BECOME even before you really BECOME that, is a way to press down full throttle on the Conviction pedal. So once you start believing that it is absolute, you need to behave accordingly. If it's the little red car that you have asked for from the Universe or the much coveted academic achievement, you should have absolute conviction in it, and make room for receiving it—may be a garage in your backyard or a defined place in your personal wall of fame to hang memories of your achievements. If it's that much awaited job for which you have just given your interview, buy new clothes and shoes to wear to the office. Or if you are waiting to get married make room in your life to accommodate that person when he/she comes to your life. Once you have conviction in your wish the whole Universe will conspire to give it to you. Don't ask why or how. That's not your lookout. Your job is to ask for it, have total clarity and conviction in it and make room to receive it.

The strength of your signals with which you follow the above given three steps determines how soon, how effectively and how wholesomely your wish will be fulfilled.

NO DOUBT = QUICK MANIFESTATION

SOME DOUBT = SLOW MANIFESTATION

LOTS OF DOUBT = NO MANIFESTATION

A very dear friend of mine used to say "You know what? Someday I will receive a presidential award. There will be a huge laminated photograph of mine in our sitting room with me receiving an award from the President of India."

We all laughed. We were than in our 6th standard and my friend was an extremely poor student. He would barely get the passing grades to make it to the next standard. His report card always showed up in red. We, on the other hand, were all under the category of 'good students'.

"For consistently having red circles in your report card?" I teased.

He was a dear friend, so he never took my teasing to heart, but what I did not know was that there was a power house of conviction in his statement that was boiling within him. With every passing year I was glad to observe that his grades improved considerably. Later, when he was doing his Masters in Botany, I went to his house one fine day and I saw a huge empty photo frame standing on his study table. I asked him what it was. He smiled and said it was for that photograph of him with the President. "And I am so excited that it is APJ Abdul Kalam. He is the best president India has ever had."

I thought my friend has lost his mind. The confidence with which he said it was even more daunting.

Then during his M. Sc. finals, once again when I went to his house the same photo frame was hanging on his sitting room wall, and still empty. This time I was really worried for him. You don't predict achievements of such huge magnitude. I mean, who wouldn't want to be awarded by the President of his country for his achievements? But his bent of conviction had a crazy edge to it . . . or so I thought. For I was wrong! Today the photo frame is adorned with our glorious President shaking hands with my very dear friend while receiving the gold medal for his excellent performance in his academic field and his overall contribution to the field of science!

He made a wish, affirmed it to the universe over and again, had total clarity about it, had conviction in it and received it by making room for it in his life. Felt it in his hand even before he had actually received it and his dream materialized. This is a simple, and yes, really very simple example of the power of mind and power of the universal energy.

4. HOPE AND FAITH

President Obama of U.S., won the election and became president just based on those two words. He gave hope to the people and showed them that they need to have faith in their own abilities. Not only had he given hope and faith to others, he was himself very hopeful and that's where the book called "Audacity Of Hope" came into existence. His subconscious had zero doubt in the ability of the universe to deliver what he wanted.

These too are very important. At no point in time can we lose hope and faith. I know these words, again, are so overtly used that they have lost its strength. They also sound like words of a weak soul. But try achieving something without either of them and see what happens.

"Hope and faith are the two strong pillars that sustain you in the gestation period of making a wish and achieving it".

It's this very hope and faith that keeps you going. These are the only two spaces which allow you to work towards your goal. If you are building your dream home, failing a million times before you make an invention or baking that chocolate cake for the first time for your loved ones, you need to keep hope alive and have faith in your wish. These terms of serenity will allow you to realize your dream and let you follow your heart, step by step, till you achieve your goal.

I would like to share that if you have followed the first 3 steps then you will automatically be able to have a great amount of hope and faith.

We have seen people conquer heaven and hell and the earth in between with this very strength that we have just discussed—

A BURNING DESIRE that is strongly supported by an **ABSOLUTE CLARITY** and **CONVICTION, HOPE** and **FAITH**.

Every time this flow chart has been followed, knowingly or unknowingly, the Universe stood up in reverence and said

SO BE IT . . .

Man wanted to cook and discovered fire! They wanted to travel faster and invented the wheel! The Wright Brothers wanted to fly like a bird and invented the aero plane! Graham Bell invented the telephone that allows us to say hello! to people on the other side of the globe! Neil Armstrong landed on the moon! And 'Teinging Norgey' climbed the Himalayas! 'Sher Shah Suri' fought and killed a tiger alone with his two bare hands! A mother tore open the mouth of a wolf when she spotted her child in its killing jaws! These are all examples of the immense power of the mind and human body. Sometimes we consciously make an effort to exercise it, sometimes we find ourselves thrown in to adverse situations and then wonder how the hell did we do it?!

Two years ago there was this news that I read in the newspaper. Now listen to this, for every word of it is true—

A heavily pregnant woman was travelling in the train. At the dead of the night she visited the train washroom. While using it her baby slipped from the womb and fell on the track below. The train was still at its deadly speed. This woman ran to the door flung it open and threw herself outside the train. The train sped by as she ran back half a kilometer and picked up her baby from the track. The iron rails, as the newspaper reported, were still burning hot. By that time the passengers had stopped the train and they rushed to the spot where the woman was still sitting.

The eyewitnesses said that the woman had the infant grabbed in her chest and was shivering profusely but it was still alive! Both of them!

This, in a nutshell, describes the meaning of commitment, of hope and faith in the proverbial impossibility that she had set out to achieve, total clarity without looking right or left, without any ifs or buts, without the slightest shred of doubt, of unwavering conviction and of course always, always the burning desire of a mother to save her new born. For what desire can be more burning than that or conviction stronger than a mother's to save her child? She knew nothing else. The signals that she had sent to the Universe were threateningly strong and the LAW OF ATTRACTION had taken time zero to say YOUR WISH IS MY COMMAND. It had gathered the impossible, moved Mother Nature and provided for her. As they say, the waters parted just for her and she walked right through!

Friends, if you would just stop for a moment and ponder over the nerve racking horrifying details of this incident you would understand the impossibility of the situation and hence the power of universal laws.

The Universe provides every time when the signals emitted have such undiluted strength. The LAW OF ATTRACTION is absolute. Its 100%! It never fails.

If you here want to contradict and say that it doesn't work for you, think again. Shift through your thought process and analyse the purity of the signals that your conscious mind generates and sends to the sub-conscious. The way you tune your RAS, you will attract only those kinds of signals. If you are sending positive signals, you will get positive results, if the signals are negative so will the results be and if it's a mixed bag than probably you need to be prepared for a surprise or a shock!

There was a person who prayed to God for years until God appeared before him and granted him three wishes. "What do you want, my son?" he asked.

The person said I want my pockets to be always jingling with the sound of money. I want to be always surrounded by pretty looking girls and I want to be amidst a hundred cars always . . . God said SO BE IT and he became a bus conductor with his bus conductor bag jingling with money, pretty girls boarded the bus on an everyday basis and since he drove through the roads, he was of course amidst hundred cars—always!!

So be specific as *"Specific Is Terrific"*!

Don't be a scatter brain and send incorrect signals to the Universe. You might just be overwhelmed by the 'TATHASTU effect'—obeyed by the LAW OF ATTRACTION.

"I love the sound of money," I want to be rich," "I want to make it big someday and get married to a nice girl and have a house somewhere . . ." are all so very arbitrary. It shows that you are probably interested in a few good things but you are committed to none. So your signals are the weakest. The LAW OF ATTRACTION said TATHASTU to whatever it could decipher.

Successful people are never ambiguous with their thought process which is evident in their communication skills. When they speak they have a sense of surety in them. They seldom talk with ifs and buts, or use fillers like 'let's see', or 'let me think' etc. They drastically cut down on their 'hmms' and 'haan's' and say clearly what they have to say. It's because, they are clear in their head. Most, if not all, successful people are very good orators. They ooze confidence when they speak, their voice soothing, tone even and trained, and whatever they say all seems to be the ultimate truth in the chosen topic. This kind of confidence is only possible when you are committed to the subject and that shows in your style of communication. You will also notice that it's a pleasure listening to most of them.

So be specific, be detailed, be sure, be committed and success will be yours even before you know it. Get rid of the cobwebs in your brain and be clear in your mind for that is the communication you held with yourself.

How do People become Rich?

Why is it that only 1% of the total population of the earth is rich? At *'Challenging Horizons'* we dedicate a special sessions on **'How Rich People Think.'** Do they think differently from the rest? Do they have a different approach or a unique attitude towards people or situations? If everything is in the mind, what does their mind consist of that's different from the others? What do you mean by rich and what was their version of rich before they became rich?

Of course like each and every person, rich people, too operate from a certain make of the mind. From the time we are born to this day, each and every moment leaves an imprint on our persona. That's what shapes us. That's what makes each one of us different from the other. Like I said earlier, there is no data lost. If we can imagine a cupboard with separate shelves, there will be one for every different aspect of our life—like one for personal life, sexual life, health, relationships, aim, goal and achievements. And then there will be one for money.

All that we can think about money is all that has been stored in the storage. If, for instance, we grew up hearing that money is bad, it's evil, for the greedy, is vulgar, leads to unhappiness, is immoral, a weak person's desire etc. than that's the attitude we will have about money.

If all our life we were taught to save money for 'the rainy day' and do not spend it, that's where we will operate for the rest of our lives. We will always be in the saving mode. Just saving mode, from whatever we earn. We will never be able to tune in to the earning mode.

If we were told that we need to 'cut our suit according to our cloth' that limiting thought will always be at work while dealing with money.

These people, no matter what they do, they never become rich. They are always struggling for that little extra that will make them comfortable. And that little extra will always be a little far away from them. A thousand dollar extra is what they aspire for all their lives. Well guess what, no matter how much they earn, they are always short of that thousand dollars. They earn to save, they avoid spending that little to train themselves that will allow them to earn more in the near future. They are mostly afraid. Their mind block prevents them from taking that calculated risk. They operate from that shelf of their storage where only limiting thoughts predominate.

On the other hand people who were taught to earn it and yet respect it, welcome it with both their hands, aspire for more and yet use it for the betterment of self and others, believe that locking it away will not make it grow, instead earning it will, trust in themselves that it's right there for them to just reach out and earn, they are somehow never in short of it. They never seem to be struggling for it either. Money seems to come easy to them.

Why?

Because rich people, think differently from others. And research says that most rich people think alike. They have a similar thinking pattern and if people aspiring to become rich can copy that thought process, they too will become rich.

Your character, thinking and beliefs are critical to the level of your success. Your wealth can grow only to the extent you grow, your energy grows, and how you evolve as a person. Your present energy level should be challenged. Your limiting thoughts should be dealt with and you should confront certain questions about your personality so as to successfully deal with it.

1. Who are you?
2. How do you think?
3. How confident are you in yourself?
4. How is your relationship with others?
5. Do you really want all that money?
6. Can you handle it?
7. How well can you handle situations and people?
8. How well can you manage your state?
9. Do you deserve richness?

Answering all these correctly are vital and will go a long way to clear your shelf and change your storage box. In that, then you need to store the ones that will allow you to liberate your thought process and push you towards success.

So, now you know that there is more to richness than just reaching out and trying your hand at a particular business.

What do you mean by rich?

Your version of rich and my version of rich and the Universe's version of rich might not be the same. You want to earn ten hundred or ten thousand or ten million in whatever currency—be specific. Put your hand on your heart and say 'by the end of this year I want to earn ten million in dollars and I am committed to it.' Don't bother how? Just commit, for until one is committed, there is hesitancy, the chance to draw back and ineffectiveness. The moment you commit yourself, providence moves too. A whole stream of events then issues from this decision of commitment, raising in one's favour unforeseen incidents; meetings and material assistance which no man could have dreamt, would have ever come his way.

This is my first book and when I thought about writing a book I didn't have inkling about how to go about publishing it. I didn't know who publishes a book. Who does the printing? How does it reach the book shelves of bookstores? Then there is the cover page to be designed, media houses to be involved, readers to be informed. I didn't know about all that. I just had this book in mind, with lots of things to share with you and a laptop resting on my knees.

But as I started writing I could feel your eyes—the readers, reading it, and loving every word of it and I went on and on, nights after nights, playing the keypad on my laptop. Words tumbled and pages after pages rolled in front of me. While doing so I spoke to friends and acquaintances about my desire and things started happening. It seems miracles happened as information regarding it started coming to me even before I searched for them.

There is a plethora of formalities to complete before a book reaches the hands of readers and I didn't know any one of them. But now as you see, you are holding this book and it's real, as much for you, as it is for me!

In other words, the Universe will assist you, guide you, support you and even create miracles for you. It will bend over backwards to support you. But first, you have to commit!

Do you ever wonder why your friends with whom you went to the same school in the same grade and are from a similar family background have a better life than yours? That today he is more successful and has more money than you? This is because while practicing power of the mind they were more committed to it than you ever were. They believed in their thoughts and had faith in the universal power which most call as God. They were more consistent than you.

If you talk to rich and successful people and pose relevant questions you will find that they have a definite thinking pattern;

1) Rich people will tell you that they are the masters of their own lives. They will be super confident when they will proclaim that they will become what they want to become. No ambiguity here.

   Poor people, on the other hand will tell you that life is destiny. It's fate. One is born with it and has no control over it. They just need to surrender, accept and fit into it.

2) Rich people will show you the prudence of taking calculated monetary risks and work towards earning more. They will explain to you the importance of it in the way of getting rich.

   Poor people will have convincing arguments about why taking any kind of monetary risks is foolishness and saving not earning money is the key to become rich.

3) Rich people dare to cut their suit larger than their cloth. In fact they dare to dream about thousands of similar suits, even when they do not have enough money for one. In short, they dare to dream big and believe in it.

Poor people think small, Period! They are miser even in the magnitude of their thoughts. They feel guilty, to think big, lest they get labelled as greedy, evil . . .

4) Rich people shift through situations and grab opportunities. Even one is good enough.

Poor people just see big boulders, the size of dinosaurs, between them and their goal.

5) Rich people, almost all of them, admire, even revere other rich people. They attract each other like magnets. They club together, dine together and share ideas.

Poor people stay away from all rich people, on principle. They can never believe that richness can come through fair means too. For them, all rich people are of dubious character and possess all the vices of the forbidden world. Poor people resent richness. Not that they are especially attracted to their fellow poor ones. They almost equally resent them too! This instinct of resentment to one and all for no particular reason is a killer trait. This makes their minds heavy as boulders.

6) Like attracts like. Rich people are mostly found in the association of other rich and successful people. You will also find them mingling with other promising young men and women, talking to them and listening to their new innovative ideas about various aspects of life.

Poor people keep their association limited to other poor ones and failures. They like to get together and talk a lot about each other's failures and wonder at life's injustice. Then have a marvellous dinner sadly and go home to brood some more.

7) Rich people like to perform. And base their rewards on the basis of their performance. They are not bothered about the time or the effort they put in and give bullshit about sympathies and empathies if the job at hand is not accomplished. They have to get the job done—successfully—before they can accept a reward.

Poor people expect to get paid after they have invested their 'valuable time'. Never mind if the work at hand is incomplete or left in a ruin. They have tried; they have put in the effort, now they need to get paid, Period!

8) Rich people like to live in abundance. They will work hard and play harder. They will finger through various opportunities of success and making money and believe that each one of them is good enough. At the same time they do not forget to enjoy. It's not just the money that lets them enjoy. It's their attitude towards it. They know that there is but just one life and they will show you how to live it. And all of them do not necessarily involve money!

Poor people forget to live. All their energy drains out in an endeavour to earn money which they finally do not and they do not believe in enjoying. They believe life is hard and that's how it is supposed to be lived. Only kids have fun with their lives. Adults are supposed to toil in it. So for them it's not just the lack of money. It's the lack of attitude. Of course it does not cost money to sit in front of the TV and have a good spell of stupid laughter with your loved ones and feel good within. But they can't. Attitude!

9) Managing the state and managing their money is the magic mantra of rich people. If they know how to make the money, they definitely know how to keep it and make it grow further.

Poor people are a poor manager of money. Even with the very little that they have, they mismanage. It's an interesting observation that they tend to spend when the amount is less even though the expenditure is unnecessary and shy away from spending big amounts even when it is necessary. For an example they will invest in dance tuition because the fee is less than a good computer coaching which is probably more important for them at that point of time in order to move ahead. Understandably the computer coaching costs more, but the dance tuition was not necessary! Poor people can never get this calculations correct. It's strange that if these people come across 'sudden' money they invariable lose it!

10) Rich people will tell you a secret, and that is—'Money attracts money'.

Poor people too will tell you their secret, which is—'work hard for money and save every paisa, you can.'

11) The fear factor—rich people take it in their stride with sweating palms and march ahead.

Poor people give life to their fear and stop midway. They do not have a 'calculated risk' in their dictionary. A risk is a risk and it's foolish to take risks. Someday, when they are rich they will think about it. Today they just can't afford it. Well guess what, these people never get their 'someday' in their calendar.

12) Most rich people appreciate change. They endorse new ideas. They are a great fan of the glittering new generation. They are open to innovations. They love the technology. They want to learn more and more.

Most poor people are a wise owl. They are bored with everything new and believe that this distorted bunch of kids will ruin the world. They hate learning anything new and believe that everything old is gold.

Rich people have one more trait which forms a solid foundation for their success. **They love themselves**.

They consciously practice . . .

SELF-LOVE.

They sleep well, eat well, groom themselves regularly, go for jogging or do work out in the gym. When they dress up in front of the mirror every day they are happy with what they see. They are super confident about their looks. They dress well and take care of themselves. They often give examples of their own personality traits, gorgeous looks and expanse of achievements. They are conscious of every aspect of their persona, proud of their achievements, confident about their dreams happy with their present and sure of their future. These people discover very early, that it's very important to feel great about oneself in order to attract great things and enjoy the laurels.

There was a time when I would stand in front of the mirror and find faults in myself. I would do that for hours together. I hated my dark complexion, my thin structure, for having no spark in my eyes or rhythm in my body. I always complained. Due to this factor I shied away from people and had a very low self-esteem. Guess what—my wish became the universe's command. People never found me interesting to talk to . . . very few people would approach me. Girls seemed to never like my company. I was mighty jealous of those people who were bright and intelligent; who spoke with confidence had magnetic personality and got special attention. This was my life then!

When I came to this wonderful city called 'Pune', I was methodically made to learn how powerful and unique I am. I learnt how blessed I am to have this wonderful life. Many don't have even this to begin with, for I had no control over it when I was born. I realized that I could have been born with some physical or mental deformity or could have been born in the bins, but God still chose to give me a better life. I started to be grateful about what I had. I started appreciating myself and calling myself a 'CELEBRITY'. I celebrated each moment of my life. Of course the credit goes to my teachers and few friends. Today I really live every moment like a king. I get lots of appreciations from people for what I am and for what I am doing. My presence inspires people and my talks help millions realise their dreams.

Why I am sharing this? Because until I realized my 'self-worth' no one valued me. Yes you got it right. Charity begins at home. You need to start doing something first and only then the entire world will join you. Don't expect the reverse.

SELF LOVE sounds an arrogant and pompous concept, but it's not. The concept is absolutely logical and useful. The attitude should be right so as not to come across as arrogant or pompous. It's a sure shot way to feel good, always. And when someone feels good, always, he or she is in a powerful magnetic field of positive energy. And being in the magical energy zone is all you need to achieve everything in life.

Yet another trait of these people, and here, not just rich but also successful people is the . . .

Quality of Communication they hold with themselves.

Successful people, maintain a quality of communication when they are in conversation with themselves, for the **quality of communication with oneself is the quality of life we lead!**

Why?

As established earlier in the book, our mind is never in vacuum. We are constantly thinking and that too at the rate of 60,000 thoughts per day, which has a definite thinking pattern. Our thoughts are the communication mode we use with ourselves. So we need to check the flow of our thoughts and give it the desired direction that will create the required signals. By required signals or desired results I don't just mean achievement, laurels and accomplishments. Quality of communication with oneself also ensures our happiness, our ability to enjoy the little things in life and make every moment, big or small a glorious moment!

If you get the time to observe a kid, or maybe a toddler playing on their own, you will understand the value of ignorance, bliss and the importance of the quality of communication.

When I first enrolled myself for computer classes in the year 1999 I was told that the basic principle of computers is this:

INPUT—PROCESS—OUTPUT

It was told that whatever you give as input, will get processed and will be shown as output. Later when I started learning and sharing about LOA and Mind Power I realized that the basic mechanism of our life is also the same. Only the right input can produce the right output. I am sure you are also aware of this simple law.

When I meet thousands of people and ask them a simple questions "HOW ARE YOU" almost all respond by saying—I AM FINE. Do you also reply the same when someone asks you this question?

If yes, have you ever thought what input are you giving to your mind? What will be the output of it? You reading this book is an indication to me that you want to be the best, you want to achieve something great, you want to be an extraordinary person and you really want to do something different. You want to be the director of your own life. But my questions is—how will you make a super hit movie with ordinary input? Can you imagine what damage you are doing to yourself by using 'ordinary' words?

"You are an idiot, you will never achieve anything, you will be a failure, you are good for nothing" as you are giving negative inputs to yourself constantly. What emotions does this line bring to you? What pictures are created by reading the first line of this paragraph? I am sure they are not too exciting and that's exactly, what you would never want.

YOU ARE AN EXTRAORDINARY PERSON WHO HAS THE POWER TO CONQUER YOUR OWN MIND AS YOU ARE BORN TO WIN! YOU BELEIVE IN YOURSELF! YOU TAKE CHARGE OF YOUR LIFE. YOU ARE AN INSPIRATION FOR MANY AND PEOPLE LOOK UP TO YOU. YOU ARE A LEADER AND A CREATOR. YOU ARE A ROCKSTAR! YOU ARE UNSTOPPABLE! YOU ARE A SHINING STAR! YOU ARE THE HAPPIEST! YOU ARE THE GREATEST! AND YOU ARE THE BEST!

How do you feel after reading this paragraph? I am sure right this moment you have a broad grin on your face. Yes that's what happens when you give yourself the right inputs. Right inputs will always help you produce the right outputs.

From now onwards when someone asks you 'How are you'? Your reply should be:

I AM GREAT
I AM EXCELLENT
I AM WONDERFUL
I AM ON TOP OF THE WORLD
I AM EXCITED
I AM SUPERB
I AM FABULOUS

As these are some of the power words which will condition your mind to produce the right outputs.

Each word which you use has a power, as it has got a certain meaning and certain vibrations attached to it. That is the reason wise people say that 'speak for others what you would like to hear for yourself' That's why people say 'what goes around comes around' Till this moment you were unaware of this fact but now you know about it. Now onwards using ordinary words for yourself and others is a crime for you, as by doing that you are just putting major road blocks in your own success.

The things that are constantly playing in our mind are the quality of life we have or aspire to have. It can never be otherwise. We cannot aspire to lead a life which is completely different from our thoughts. Are we constantly competing and comparing with someone else? Do we spend a lot of time thinking about achieving things merely to show off? Are we jealous of our friend's success or our fellow brothers' laurels? Are we constantly contemplating misgivings for others? Then our Quality of communication with self is very raw and uneducated. It's undignified and cheap. And if this is what consist our thought process, this is what we will receive from the Universe.

"Improving the Quality of Communication with self . . .
will go a long way in making you a very happy person"

So now we have 12 definite pointers and self-love to becoming rich. We have also understood the concept of the Quality of Communication with self.

What do we do now? We think about these pointers and initiate a change within ourselves. We need to see which category we fall in and decode the secret behind our thinking process.

Knowing all these will not suffice. They will give you a definite platform and a starting point. These things need to be **implemented** and to begin with, you need to be open to change. Take each one up and discard the ones you think is detrimental to your growth. You need to keep your mind open and try out the new . . .

Practicing power of the mind, commanding your thought process and emitting distilled positive energy to the Universe is easier said than done. Human beings are a creature of habits. It's difficult to break an old thought process or get into a new one. There will always be an element of resistance. And these resistances are the . . .

Weakening black threads in your bold red road of desire.

People, who are committed to their dreams, eliminate or at least try to lessen as much as possible, of those useless black weakening threads. They overcome them; make a huge dent into old habits and make a head way. *How?* That's the power of commitment. Provided you understand the meaning of commitment. So, do this—stand up from where ever you are sitting, place a hand on your chest and say 'I am committed to start this business of mine by the end of this year or score 98 per cent in my exams" or whatever it is that you desire!

Have you done it?

No?

.

.

.

.... still no?!

If you think this practice is weird? Then my friend, you are still not into the bracket. You have some more work to do.

Thinking an act as 'weird' or an idea 'stupid' are all resistances of the mind. Once you are committed to your dreams you will find clearing these very blocks, easy. Ego hassles, stubbornness, jealousy, back-biting, bitching, unnecessary small talks, negative talks, talks of diseases or illness are different examples of mind block. If you interact with people placed high in their life, who are successful and achievers, you will realise that they never indulge in petty talks of jealousy, misunderstanding and ego hassles. They have freed themselves of such slow poisoning. They don't let such negative thoughts cloud their mind and dilute their concentration. They keep the black threads to the minimum. They are all aware! Those people of the yesteryears, they all knew the magnetic power of the energy field around . . . Einstein, Graham Bell, Neil Armstrong, and also 'Aryabhatt' who introduced the stupid, useless, valueless 'zero' and forever changed the world of mathematics—they knew everything. They never thought any act as weird. They allowed themselves to do a million stupid things until they made their discoveries and inventions and changed the earth. Today we all know who they are and what their names stand for!

Why am I mentioning these names to you? Because before they started off to achieve something, they got rid of these mind blocks. Standing up in front of the mirror and saying something is not important. But finding it so utterly impossible to do something so simple is the mind block. You can't do this act because you have never done something like this before. This is part of a habit—of not being able to do something, so simple . . . just because you have never done it before.

Honestly, even if you try to do it, later, when I am not breathing down your neck forcing you to do it, you will still find it very difficult. You will be extremely uncomfortable, with this 'weird' act and keep feeling awkward throughout the day. You will find it absolutely unbelievable that you have actually done something so stupid after reading a book!

This very discomfort is a part of the habit of doing or not doing something. Breaking it seems so uncomfortable that you quickly want to undo it and get back to where ever you were. And that's where the power of commitment comes in. It makes you break through everything, do the impossible and achieve your dreams.

No wish is weird enough or dream impossible with the power of universe. It makes things happen, just like that.

Almost two years back I was invited to my friend's house for lunch. Her elder sister too was there at that time, holidaying with her two children. I was delighted to see her! It had been years since we met. While eating, I noticed that she was barely nibbling at her food. She was toying with the serving spoon and pushing the food around in her plate. From our previous acquaintance I know she is a voracious eater and loves her food. I asked her what happened. Is she unwell? She laughed and replied that she is perfectly fine. Just that after two kids she has put on too much of weight and so is trying to check her diet.

"Who says you are fat?"

"Well, I can see myself in the mirror and everyone says so."

'Then from now on every time you look into the mirror' say 'I am thin. I have the perfect body that I always wanted and nothing is wrong with me.' Say this every morning when you wake up and before going to bed. Say this before every meal you eat. Try and wear beautiful clothes with a perfect fit and some preferred cosmetic like your eye kohl or your lip gel when you sit for your meal. Say this whenever you are feeling low and fat. Imagine yourself in the body of the diva you currently admire and buy clothes exactly the size you want to be."

"And waste all that money?! You must be crazy! What good would imagination do?"

"Try it," I insisted, "Try it for at least six months. Write in a piece of paper the exact vital statics that you want and paste it in front of the mirror. Keep a measuring tape and measure yourself every day. Believe in it and make room for it. How? By buying clothes of that desired size. No matter what people say, see yourself in perfect shape and size. Eating does not make you fat. Thinking fat does. Once you really start thinking about yourself as nice and slim you will be granted your wish.'

I met my friend's sister two months later and she was elated with the results. She said this is the first time in her entire life that she is happy with her body and so is her measuring tape! She is wearing the clothes she always wanted to wear but never could. She said she just could not believe that mere thoughts could make so much of difference.

Some people are diagnosed with slow thyroid. Some people are told that their bodies have a slow metabolism rate. Then there is the hereditary factor. For women, pregnancy and child birth plays a big role in toppling their desired body weight. These people are conditioned to think fat. Once you accept any of these factors applicable to you, and you believe in it, you start putting on weight. You then think it's a natural condition and you are powerless against it. You become fatter. You lose hope. But to apply the LAW OF ATTRACTION it's so important that

'In order to lose weight you have to start off—by thinking 'thin thoughts'.

It is impossible to lose weight while thinking 'fat thoughts' simultaneously. It completely defies the LAW OF ATTRACTION. You must feel good about yourself, about your body, your hair, skin, your eyes, the clothes you wear and the way you look. Every time you look into the mirror, it is imperative that you see a beautiful person in the reflection.

During my 8th standard in school I used to go to a math professor for private tuitions. He took tuitions in batches and we were a batch of six boys and girls. There was one girl I remember from our tuition group. Why? Because I met her again a few days back on a fluke chance in a restaurant. Back then there was nothing special about her for me or anyone to remember. She was a very annoying character. She was irritating in her disposition and always ready to defend herself even when there was no challenge. She wasn't exactly ugly, but her presence was a definite put-off. She was the only petulant character in the entire group. The rest of us were good friends. I know it is very unethical to talk about a person in this tone but there is a reason for it and I want to share it with you, especially my women readers.

That day at the restaurant when she said hi! to me all of a sudden, I was so surprised. Is this the same person? How come she is looking beautiful?! She was actually looking so gorgeous that I couldn't stop myself from complimenting her. But what intrigued me was the way she received it. Before she thanked me for the compliment showered on her, she said 'yes, I know', which meant 'yes, I know I am beautiful, and thank you.' The style was a little unconventional. Her smile was pleasant, her face radiant and those eyes, which, back then, had the potential to give you a night long nightmare (Sorry), now were twinkling with life, rarely seen. I had to ask her to sit down and talk to me for some time. It wasn't just past acquaintance. The change in her persona was of herculean magnitude. I knew there had to be something in it. Something more and I wanted to know—

"I stay in Bangalore these days," she said. "Four years back I attended a session of yours that you had conducted in Bangalore."

"You did?!" I said, truly surprised. "Why didn't you walk up to me after the session?"

"I had sent you several e-mails" she said and smiled.

"But I do reply to e-mails."

"You did. But you did not recognize me. But that's not the point. The point is attending those sessions of yours has changed my life completely and that's what's there in those e-mails." She laughed a beautiful crystal clear laugh.

I wanted to know more and asked her if she could share with me what happened that has brought In, this pivotal change in her.

She shared—her story—

She was born an ugly duckling—small, black, shrunken, underweight and a head full of curly hair. Her mother had a tough time to keep her alive till she was two years old. In her growing years she was constantly teased for her ugly looks—Good naturedly by her cousins and unkindly by schoolmates and friends. Of course at that tender age she did not find any goodness in that nature of teasing nor did she have the mental strength to rebut the jibes of her friends.

She was always made to stand in the last row of the school choir band; she was kept as an extra in her school basketball team even though she played well. At the home front she felt her mother always picked up ugly clothes for her and she was not allowed to use any makeup because it did nothing for her. When cousins went out together, they refused to allow extra time for her to get ready.

"Wear anything. How does it matter?"

All these had a profound effect on her. Every time she looked into the mirror her horrifying ugly reflection stared back. Her clothes were always shabby, the cut wrong and the color never suited her no matter how many different shades she tried.

If someone was good to her, she always thought that they had some ulterior motives to it. When someone was bad she fought with them relentlessly and without any dignity.

She anyways never believed she had any.

At the school when teachers pulled her up for low grades or incorrect work or late attendance she always thought they shouted at her a little more cruelly only because she was ugly. She never tried to be nice to anyone. What's the use? No one was nice to her. She was a total misfit to the society. Life was difficult for her and she had to live it. So she had waged a war against it. All around was a battle ground.

After attending my sessions, she said, she found so many things I had said were true. She could personally relate to many examples that I had shared in the workshop. She then took time to think over the things that I had said during the session. "Why don't you write a book about all the stuff that you yank of? That way I will not have to tax my memory chip. I can open it anytime I want to read and skip read." She had then said, between her narrations.

*She said after my session's one thing hit her hard as a boulder—she was so loathsome about herself that she was indeed **blocking all good things coming towards her!** How could anyone love her when she herself hated her so much!? There was nothing positive about her. Every thought of her was negative. She believed everything turned in the opposite direction from her and if she had to achieve it she had to fight. Nothing in this world was meaningful for her.*

After attending my sessions she realized that life was indeed difficult for her because she made it so, with her own thoughts and wishes. She defied every rule in the rule book of the LAW OF ATTRACTION and then expected to attract good things towards her! And then blamed destiny and her ugly looks when things did not turn out as per her wishes!

What catastrophe!!

How could she look beautiful when she felt so ugly? How could anyone fall in love with her when she hated herself so much? How could she be happy, when all her thoughts were sad? How could good things come her way when she saw only bad things all around her?

Once she got a drift of the flow of her thoughts she was amazed to realise, what she was doing to herself. She knew she had to stop. A complete full stop and make a U-turn. She wrote down all her thoughts—positive and negative and analysed them.

She vowed to herself that every time she looked into the mirror she will see someone beautiful. She would then first stand in front of the mirror and say thank you for a perfect body—her two hands, two legs, two eyes, her lips and nose, her long hair and perfect height. Her skin, she observed was flawless and her voice sweet. Wow!! She never really noticed all this ever before! She was indeed beautiful, she made herself think and the clothes she wore were great!

With each passing day she admired herself more and more and then something happened which had never happened before. She got the first compliment of her life! From an office colleague! That colleague said she was looking very different today and that she was looking beautiful! And then again, a few days later from another of one of her colleagues and again and again—till she got used to it.

The world became a little bit more tolerable and things started coming easy to her—like an invitation to a get-together at a friend's place, which never happened before or a secret admirer she had no knowledge of! She was also asked to host the show of the upcoming annual office activity! She was thrilled with everything that was going around. Suddenly life became real and she found herself surrounded with happiness.

And then one fine day the unthinkable happened. The man of her dream proposed to her! He was one of the most handsome guy around and also the most eligible. She had always secretly admired him but never gave the possible relation a thought. But now that she realized she was beautiful she dared to make the wish.

And what did the Universe say? You are right. So Be It!

And it's not just about your coveted vital statistics, or how beautiful or ugly you are or your dream man or woman. Did you know that today doctors are actively doing research on alternative curing methods? And one of the streams of such research is by activating the power of mind and thereby triggering cure? Where is the science, you may ask? So here it goes—

The building unit of a body is a cell. Cells in the body are replaced on a daily basis. Old cells give way to new ones. Those are the dead cells which we scrub off with a scrubber to look nice and fresh. We find a plethora of such scrubbers in the market. Organs too are made of cells and they too keep regenerating new ones. So, going by this theory we have a brand new organ to flaunt every few weeks! So, then, medically if one gets affected by some disease it anyway gets replaced from time to time.

Then? What gives?

Why does one person die of a certain disease that the other gets cured of? How come 'Yuvraj Singh' is back in the field with renewed burst of life and vibrancy? One look at him and you might think that he has come back from a chance encounter with flu or a long holiday in the Mediterranean! He definitely doesn't look like someone who has fought cancer. We have all seen too many of such patients and we all know what they look like.

What are medical miracles? How does it happen? And why doesn't it happen to everyone? Is it that God doesn't love everyone equally!?

God loves 'Yuvraj Singh' more or 'Liza Ray' more who had survived terminal breast cancer, than us? Where is the missing link?

The missing link is in the conviction part of it and then receiving. For some weird reason most people believe, or rather like to believe, that they are dying. Even when they are down with the seasonal flu! They will exaggerate their illness, cough a little more, whine a little longer and look out for sympathetic shoulders. It sure feels good to have someone pamper you when you are not in your best, but please do remember that that's exactly what you are asking for from the universe. By the LAW OF ATTRACTION, what you concentrate on expands. So by concentrating on your illness, in order to attract attention, you are only attracting more of the lethargy. So long it's the seasonal flu, its fine. But 'I am not well' syndrome might attract more of it and in different variety, for which you might not be prepared for!

'Yuvraj Singh' and 'Liza Ray' did not survive because God loves them more than us. They survived because they had Conviction and Faith in their recovery. They did not waste time thinking how terribly sick they were. Instead they constantly thought of getting back to their respective fields. They did the needful, went through the treatment and said 'bullshit' to their illness, while they lived every moment ushering the time when he would march to the field amidst roaring and cheering crowd and she would walk down the ramp looking like a diva.

The Universe said 'You Will Get It!'

Have you ever noticed that people who complain of bad health are almost always ailing? They will always have something or the other to complain about. On the other hand there are some people who are never sick.

Poor people never complain of illness. In their mind they dread illness. For them doctor and medicine means money! Which they do not have. So they con themselves by believing that nothing is wrong with them. Well more often than not they prove themselves right. Poor people do die old, without paying huge medical bills year on year, braving the atrocities of life and work hard to earn their daily breads. How do they manage to do that? They do that by conniving with the LAW OF ATTRACTION to keep them in their pink of health so that they can keep working and earning their daily breads for themselves and their family.

They avoid diseases with big fat stylish names just by being ignorant about them. They can't attract something they don't have knowledge of.

The LAW OF ATTRACTION says you will get what you want!

Doctors too, usually keep a medicine called **PLACEBO**. These are nothing but sugar pills and can do no harm to the body. For people who are in the habit of thinking themselves ill, it's for them. Doctors, especially family physicians, follow the pattern. Most headaches, backaches, perceived fever are more of the working of the mind than real illness. When doctors recognise such pattern and prescribe the medicine these perceived illnesses vanish! It's all in the mind and that's what the physician targets while treating such patients. They believe that their illness is cured by the medicine. And so they are cured.

Very busy people too are seldom ill. You will never hear them complaining about headache, stomach ache or fever. They are never down with the weather or out with a fever. They just don't have time for all these. So the LAW OF ATTRACTION too complies with them and says YOU CREATE YOUR DESTINY

Do you know that people with problematic eyesight are now advised to encourage their eyes to correct themselves? To make an effort to see without an aid! You need to believe that there is nothing wrong with your eyes and that your eye sight is perfect. Researchers have observed that if the eye does not have any disease like Glaucoma, or cataract or infection as such but just a sight issue, it gets corrected by awareness and mind power.

Doctors, after observing the results of mind power, once said that if we could prescribe prayers in the prescription, we would have done so. Medicines are as effective on a body as the patients will it to. Probably that's one of the reasons, if not all the reason, why the same pill has varying degree of effect on different patients.

If placebo is used by doctors to con the mind of patients who don't know the power of the mind, people with real illnesses use this very awareness to cure themselves of life threatening illness. Such stories about medical miracles can fill up a big fat book and every story will affirm the power of the mind.

We have heard stories about near death experience and we also today know what the **tunnel of death** looks like. People who have returned from death describe dropping through an unending tunnel of light and dark and some colors. Their description is very similar to each other which gives us knowledge of how the last journey looks like or feel like.

We have by now very well established the power of the mind and what it can achieve with some technique and lots of awareness.

Most of us fear the future. Fear of the unknown, unseen!

That's how we have been conditioned since birth. We have been methodically seasoned to secure our future. But seldom did anyone tell us to live our today. For that's all we have—Today. It is said that tomorrow is an uncertainty and yesterday is gone. Today is when we should live, like it is the last day or the first day of our lives. To most of us, it sounds all nice and peppy but extremely impractical. We bull head to secure the future and do whatever it takes to do that. We forget our dreams. Dreams are a fool's plaything. We work, we earn, we live a lavish life but most of us are still unhappy.

My endeavour through **IGNITING THE SPARK** is to make people aware of the core thing that will make them happy. To help find them their individual source of happiness, because most of us search happiness in the wrong place. Arbitrarily pick up someone else's dream and try and make it our own. Like wanting to become a doctor or an engineer because it's an easily available option or because everyone does so. Power of mind tells you that dreams are real and each and every **realistic dream** is meant to be materialized if we abide by the LAW OF ATTRACTION.

So I would like to stress upon a few points that will assure you that no dream is futile and no fear real.

The first point I want to discuss, a little bit in detail, is the concept of **BURNING DESIRE**. For that's where 'living' begins—with a burning desire.

I have talked about burning desire earlier in the book. We all know what it is. The moment you hear this word, a few of your own pops out in your mind and probably your eyes glaze with a sigh. An 'if only . . .' expression masks your face for everyone to see. So we are well versed with this expression of BURNING DESIRE.

But how do we fuel our burning desire?

Do we at all know that it is something to be consciously done or else it reaches no further than just a feeble want?!

From time to time we all want something or the other. Sometimes some of these wants are met, sometimes not. We are mostly ok with that. But only if we consciously practice the concept of 'BURNING DESIRE', each of these wants can be fulfilled. Yes, and there are ways to do it.

We first need to

'Fuel our Desires every day'.

How to Fuel your Desires

I really had this desire to write this book. But this was not a burning desire as I was not able to fuel this desire enough to keep it burning. Many a times I thought about it but didn't follow through. 31st December 2012 I sat for setting my next year's goals. I wrote in my diary that I am super excited as it's the 31st of December 2013 and I am holding my book in my hand. I could achieve my goal on 1st of November 2013 and today you are holding this book and my desire is a reality. Do you know how to fuel your desires? Here are some powerful ways which I have been following and sharing with many. I am sure you will love this part of the book the most, as this is where most of the people fail.

AFFIRMATIONS

Having heard this many times I am sure you are wondering about its true meaning—so here it goes: "Affirmations are positive statements! Statements that describe a desired situation, and which are repeated many times, in order for the same to register in the subconscious mind and bring about a positive action."

Key aspects to ensure that affirmations are effective would be—attention, conviction, interest and desire.

Imagine that you are running with your friends around a football field. They run ten rounds, something you have never done before, and as you want to win their respect, you want to show them that you can make it too. You start running, and at the same time keep repeating in your mind, "I can do it, I can do it . . ." You not only think but also believe that you are going to complete those ten rounds. What are you actually doing? You are repeating positive affirmations.

Many of us repeat in our minds, words and statements concerning the situations and events in their lives—negatively! And consequently, create situations that are not desirable. Words and statements work both ways, to build or to destroy. It is the usage of these, which determines whether they are going to bring good or harmful results.

Many a times, people repeat negative statements in their minds, without even being aware of what they are doing. Do you keep thinking and telling yourself that you cannot do something, you are too lazy, lack inner strength, or that you are going to fail? Your subconscious mind accepts these as the wholesome truth and eventually attracts corresponding events and situations into your life, irrespective of whether they are good or bad for you. So why not choose only positive statements?

Affirmations are to humans; what commands and scripts are to computers: They program the mind in the same way that commands and scripts program a computer. The repetition of words help your mind focus on your goal, and automatically build corresponding mental images in the conscious mind, which influence the subconscious mind, similar to how 'creative visualization' works. The conscious mind, the mind you think with, starts this process, and then the subconscious mind takes charge. By using this process intentionally, you can influence your subconscious mind, and transform your habits, behavior, mental attitude, and reactions, and even reshape your life.

Results are not always immediate. Sometimes it requires more time. Various factors determine this, like time, focus, faith and feelings you invest in repeating your affirmations, on the strength of your desire, and on how big or small is your goal.

A word of caution here though, even if you are repeating positive affirmations for a few minutes but then continue thinking negatively more often the rest of the day, the effect of positive words is neutralized! IF you want results—you just need to refuse to think negatively.

Repeating Affirmations

It is best to repeat affirmations that are short, and makes them easy to remember. One great way to ensure that you repeat affirmations often . . . is to repeat them every time your mind is not engaged in something important, such as while traveling in a bus or a train, waiting in line, walking, etc., but do not affirm while driving or crossing a street. Repeating them in special sessions of 5-10 minutes each, several times a day can get you the desired results faster.

Being relaxed both physically and mentally while affirming strengthens the concentration, the more faith you have in what you are doing, the more emotions you put into the act, the stronger and faster will be the results.

Choosing only positive words while describing what you really want is important. If you want to lose weight, do not tell yourself "I am not fat" or "I am losing weight." These are negative statements and bring into the mind mental images of what you do not want. Say instead, "I am getting slim" or "I have reached my perfect weight". Such words bring positive images in the mind.

Always be in the present while you affirm. Use sentences in the present tense, not the future tense. Saying, "I will be successful", means that you intend to be successful one day, in the undefined future, but not now. It would be more effective to say, and feel, "I am successful now", and the subconscious mind will work overtime to make this happen now, in the present.

The power of affirmations can help you to transform your life. By stating what you truly want in your life, you mentally and emotionally see and feel it as true, irrespective of your current circumstances, and thereby attract it into your life.

Positive Affirmations

I am healthy and Wealthy.

Riches are pouring into my life.

I am riding on the road of wealth.

I am getting wealthier each day.

My body is healthy and functioning at its best.

I have abundant energy.

I learn and comprehend fast.

My mind is calm.

I am always calm and relaxed.

My thoughts are under my control.

I radiate love and happiness.

I am living in the house that I want.

I have good and loving relation with my wife/husband.

I have a wonderful and satisfying job.

I am successful in whatever I do.

Everything is getting better every passing day.

An Abraham Hicks Technique—17 seconds

This technique says that if we can put in 17 seconds of pure undiluted thought towards the achievements of our goal three to four times in a day we have done a great job and that we are spearheading towards success. Abraham further says that 17 seconds of pure thoughts are equal to 2000 action hours. 34 seconds of pure intention is as powerful as 20000 action hours and if this duration is increased to 68 seconds then the energy multiplies and holds the power equal to 200000 action hours. You must be surprised to hear these numbers but it's the truth as this is how certain people attract all the good things in life without even constantly working for them.

Why 17 seconds? Because that's the maximum time span we can hold an undiluted thought. We humans, almost all of us, cannot finish a sentence without contradicting it then and there. And that's within less than 2 seconds. This sends mixed signals and our goals are pushed further away. For an example we say "I really want this new car, but it's so expensive that it's impossible to get it".

Abraham says that a pure undiluted thought holds good for 17 seconds after which it burns out and gives birth to another thought. Because this 'another-thought' is a new fresh one, it is more powerful than the previous one which by now is exhausted. So the new thought, by the LAW OF ATTRACTION, will have the power or a higher energy level. If for some reason the second thought is negative and contradictory to the first one, the first one will be nullified by it.

So now that we know it, we should have 3-4 sessions of pure thoughts and consciously not follow it up with negative contradictory thoughts. If we can manage 34 seconds or 68 seconds total for a day we have done great for ourselves.

So how do we get 17 seconds of pure undiluted thoughts? For most of us it is impossible to sit and think something for a span of 17 seconds and not pepper it with say a dash of Pizza-thought, if they are hungry or an unimportant traffic thought if they are already late! Or maybe they are pushing a deadline at work which is always a more dominating thought.

Write it down . . . And be as detailed and articulate as possible. Create a dimension. If your thought is for a new house, imagine it in detail. The rooms and bedrooms, the colour of the paint, the kitchen, the sitting area, the living room, balcony and terrace, the colour and texture of the draperies, the door knobs, the bathroom faucets, the electrical attachments, which brand to prefer, which shops to visit, what furniture to choose, where to place them. Try and chalk out inch by inch detail of it. Even find the place for hanging the keys and placing the shoe rack. This will tax your entire attention and tug hard at your conscious and sub-conscious mind demanding your full attention. So here you will get your 17 seconds of pure undiluted thoughts.

Harness the Power of Incantation

When you are angry ... When you are fearful ... When you are ecstatic ... When you are jumping with joy ... What are you doing? You are practicing INCANTATION at those times.

You must be wondering what that is. The dictionary meaning of the word incantation is **"the chanting or uttering of words purporting to have magical power"** That's when your **FEELINGS**, your **ACTIONS** along with your **WORDS, EMOTIONS** and **THOUGHTS** about that particular dream are all in the same direction.

Yes when you speak a word with feeling, action, emotions and apply the right tone to it—it gets the power to really attract things faster in your life, because that's the moment when all these 5 elements have congruency. When your thoughts, feelings, actions, words and tone of voice all are in sync that is the time, you are operating with pure energy and your frequency is the highest. This is the time your attraction power is the highest.

When you are out to achieve something it is vital that you are in total control of yourself—your body, mind and soul are in Congruence. You should not be in their control.

Avoid **'monkey personality'** at all cost.

What is a **'monkey personality'**?

People whose behaviour dances to the external conditions. Who reacts to people and situations! An annoying person makes you annoyed, an irritating character makes you irritated, bad situation makes you angry, and failure frustrates you. When someone appreciates you, it makes you happy and a criticism can ruin your day. You make yourself a **monkey** to the surrounding. Your reactions to minutes are way out of your control. Your life is a puppet in the hands of people, situations and characters and NOT YOU. Incantation by such personalities does not come easy. Incantation, even for 17 seconds, needs huge mind power and a monkey personality, whose mind is always in the grip of someone else or something else, finds it difficult to bring all his emotions to a convex point. **Managing the State** means exactly that. No matter what the external environment is, you need to manage your state at all cost. Getting swayed by emotions and forgetting everything else or getting into a grip of anger and losing your self-control are detrimental to you and your health.

All great people are masters of this art. You will never spot a great name exposing his radical mood to the world around. They can always manage their state. They are always practicing Incantation. It comes to them naturally. They don't have to force themselves into it. And when they are in Incantation everything in them are **CONGRUENT** with each other and in the same energy frequency.

FEELINGS+ACTIONS+WORDS+EMOTIONS+THOUGHTS = INCANTATION.

What are feelings?

Feelings are the **'thermometers of your thoughts'**

Having said that we need to understand that we have to inculcate positive thoughts to send positive signals to the universe and have positive results, and that negative thoughts are detrimental to the realization of those very dreams. We now know that we have some 60,000 odd thoughts in a day! Now, how the hell do we monitor all of them? Is it possible? Probably not! So we consult our feelings. If you are feeling good, your flow of thoughts is definitely positive. If you are not feeling good within yourself than the thought process must be negative. It means we need to do something immediately to pull up our mood. Tune back again to the frequency of positive signals and then try and keep on track.

Positive feelings have the potential to trigger positive actions, lots of positive words and emotions, lots of love with the ambience around, and also trigger positive thoughts and happiness. When you are in this zone, you are in perfect congruent with the universe. Your signals are the strongest and the universe says YOUR WISH IS MY COMMAND.

Power of Visualization

Visualization has proved to be a very powerful concept and extremely effective, if we do it with loads of dedication.

If it's that exorbitantly priced new car that you have seen doing the streets these days go head and visualize it. Search up information about it in the latest magazines and newspaper. Look up for it on the internet. If possible go and visit the showroom and try sitting inside one of them right there. Take a test drive. Touch it, feel it. Energize it so much that even if you are driving your old car it feels like the new one you are dreaming about. And with people who don't drive a car, there should be no reason not to fantasize it. The idea is not to go paranoid about it but to make it a part of your everyday life. Be comfortable with it. Eat, live and sleep with it. Your wish will be granted to you.

What does being comfortable here mean? It means that the idea should not sit like an elephant, sitting in your thousand square feet two bedroom apartment! Watching TV and sipping coke!

Many people have read this concept and have also followed it up to some extent; however most get disappointed and give it up as they don't see instant results. So here are few things for you to follow this process of visualization and bring results out of it.

1. Universe doesn't have the concept of time. Time is created by humans for their own understanding of day and night and to calculate their life span. You can't expect from universe that your dream car or dream home should come to you in a day or in a year. Universe responds to the frequency of your feelings and intensity of your desire. Low intensity + Low frequency = slower results and vice versa. Hence don't ask universe how long it will take to materialize your desires. Instead just keep on visualizing till you get the results. The beauty is that the more you follow with heart the faster the manifestation would be.

2. Don't just visualize, enjoy the process and be joyful while doing this activity. Visualization should give you goose bumps. When you visualize you should have a broad smile on your face, your body should be in the same position in which it would be if your desire have already come true, and your breathing pattern should also be matching to the desired breathing pattern.

   You can't fool your mind ever. If you visualize without feelings then your mind will never agree to it. Hence feeling is the most important part of your visualization.

   The key is that—there should not be any difference in your desired physical and mental state and the current physical and mental state. If your current frequency of thoughts and feelings can match your desired frequency of thoughts and desires then the attraction would be happening at a great speed

3. If you want something from your parents, friends or anyone and you ask him once or twice its fine. But if you keep nagging them they will get frustrated, as either they will feel you don't trust them or you are mad. Nobody loves a nag. In both ways their behaviour towards you will be negative. Don't keep

visualizing throughout the day. The ideal way is to visualize only twice in a day—once in the morning and once at night before you sleep. If you keep visualizing throughout the day then you are holding this to you and not letting it float in the entire universe. That also communicates to the universe that you don't trust its ability. This will slow down the entire process of manifestation. So visualize it once or twice and then let go . . .

4. Visualize out of love and don't' try to control your mind when it's visualizing. Let it flow—Flow in its own rhythm and flow in its own speed. Remember that mind doesn't like force. Don't create any image forcefully. Be happy with what comes to your mind. Accept it. Just direct the flow but don't control the flow. Your mind is more intelligent than what you think it is. Hence believe in it and its powers will be unleashed.

Stop Desperation! Now

Some time ago, in one of my workshops a girl asked me—"Sir, many a times it happens that I want things and I work for them also. They are my burning desires and I do everything to turn them into reality but still it doesn't work—why does it happen?"

She was shocked to hear my reply. I said—"What you call as your burning desire—I call it desperation". I explained further that when you are desperate you are not happy and your happiness depends upon you achieving that end result. When you are working for a goal with lot of unhappiness, then what are you attracting? You are attracting few more reasons to be unhappy and that's the reason, when you are desperate for something, either it takes a very long time to materialize or it doesn't at all.

Most people don't get what they want in spite of putting lot of efforts and energy, because they don't remain happy in the process and they don't feel the joy of doing the things. They do the things mechanically and are desperate for the end result.

Desperation is a negative state and has got low frequency. It's like wishing to buy 1000 rupees stuff with just 50 bucks in the pocket.

You must have observed that people rarely get the things they want, when they are in the dire need of it. For an example:

If you leave your existing job and search for another job you will have lot of difficulty in finding a new one. Whereas, if you are already in a job and then search for a new job, you might get many offers in the short run. Have you experienced this or know about someone experiencing it?

There is a very thin line between desperation and burning desire. If you become aware of that then you will always be a magnet who will be able to attract anything and everything.

Be happy and move smoothly towards your goals. Enjoy the process. If you are able to enjoy the process then the destination may not matter at all. This is the way of living and only few could master this art of living.

LET GO! GET MORE!

On the occasion of Shri Krishna Janmashthamii, I went to see the function of Dahi-Handi. It is the function where people make a human pyramid by climbing on top of each other and then are supposed to snatch the pot containing curd and butter. I was observing the entire process and could realize that the person who was climbing up had to let go his fear of falling. You can only climb up if you let go of what you are holding on to.

The process of manifesting becomes very fast only when you learn to let go. If you let go of your past grudges, past challenges, past programming and the past results, only then, can you move on to the higher and better future.

On one hand you may have a burning desire but on the other hand you are holding on to trivial things, which will always pull you down and stop you from achieving what you are capable of.

It's like you have the desire to drive Mercedes Benz but you are stuck with your old Bajaj Chetek scooter.

Here are 10 powerful steps which can help you let go of your past, unimportant things and also help you focus on something which is better and brighter:

1. **Meditation:** Helps find tranquility, peace. It is an action. Fact is our body can be brought to a still state much easier than getting our mind to such a state. Reason is our lives are super-fast paced, flooded with external noise and distractions. Clarity comes from quiet and from within. Meditation is the process of reaching this quite—deep within . . . helping you dive within!

2. **Understanding:** Don't Judge, but try and reflect upon your past as an unbiased third person. Purely observe! Realize that you are not your past. Understand that the situations and people in your life created your experiences, and those experiences are not YOU nor did they create you. Knowing and understanding your past and some of your patterns will help you to recognize why you hold on and repeat self-destructive behaviors. Understanding creates awareness; awareness helps you break the cycle.

3. **Acceptance:** Accept your past and the people that have been a part of your past; accept your circumstances and with the knowledge that none of these define you. Acceptance is the first step to let go and setting yourself free.

4. **Empty your cup:** Do it, because it creates space for new experiences, new achievements and new perspective! Deliberately and proactively work at letting go!—Of your experiences; your judgments and ideals, the material things, all your 'stuff'. As they have no 'real' value. It's a myth that it makes you stronger, healthier or more powerful! Empty your expectations of how, who, where and what you should be as

they, too, are part of 'that', which holds you back from 'simply being'. Once you let go—your life will be more purposeful.

5. **Alignment:** Do you know what your core values, life purpose/ goals and action plan to achieve them are?

If not, take a moment to reflect and jot down the same. Done? If not, do take more time—in fact take all the time you need— you are definitely worth it . . .

Done?

Great! Look at your core values and do a re-check to see if they are in sync with your purpose/goals and your action plan! If the answer is a 'no', maybe it is time to create new core beliefs or goals or maybe new action plans? Jot down as many new actions that you would like to undertake.

6. **Flexibility:** It seems ironical to detach from outcomes, when you have to set goals and work toward them. Flexibility—in the right areas—like willingness to let go of the result is important. Learn to be flexible; allow the plan to flow as it will, for in the flow many an opportunity come into our lives.

7. **Giving:** Past events and experiences have a tendency to hurt or upset us. When faced with such a situation . . . try 'giving' . . . making someone else's day bright! Maybe smiling at someone as you pass, opening a door, putting in a bit extra in the CRY donation box, and giving food to the needy: can have lasting impact and help you to put your situation into perspective. Giving—to create a sense of well-being for others is the best way to align with your Inner self.

8. **Believing in self:** Belief in your existence, your purpose. Believe that the universe is unfolding as it should and that you have a divine role to play in this unfolding!

9. **Loving the Living:** Be happy. Have fun. Be a player, full of cheer and positivity. Give power to positivity. Love yourself, love others and love this life. Life is a gift for you to unwrap each and every day, to gaze upon with new and excited eyes.

10. **Gratitude and Being True to Self:** Having lived the above, just be filled with gratitude and be yourself.

Focus on Giving

Give and you shall receive, Givers always gain. You must have heard these phrases even as a child. When you give more you receive more. When you give you can expect the unexpected.

During my work at 'Symantec', I developed a habit of meeting all the people, before I sat at my seat. I continued this ritual during my association with the organisation.

When I used to shake hand with everyone I often came across a colleague of mine called "Amey S". Amey was a very nice guy and good with people, but I couldn't understand why he never responded to my wishes very enthusiastically. He kind of ignored me. Whenever I offered him my hand he never looked at me and the smile was missing from his face. I didn't like it but I still continued the same. We worked together in the same assignment for close to 14 months but he never changed.

It was my last day in that particular department as I was being moved to another in the same organization. My office location was also to be changed. On my last day Amey walked up to me and told me that he wants to have a word with me. Both of us went out and started chit chatting. All of sudden Amey said: 'Bhupendra, I know I have never spoken to you much and never responded to you the way I should have. Do you know the reason behind it?" I said 'no I don't know about it'. He said 'the reason is because I don't like people coming from other states and taking up the jobs of our people'. He said that 'the people who come from other states make fun of us and do not respect our culture and our tradition. They don't value us the way they should have been valued. Hence I am against all of them and that was the reason I was against you also.'

He continued: "but today I must say that you have won my heart. People like you are required in this state of Maharashtra. If you ever need any support, please let me know. Never ever leave Pune. We need you Bhupendra."

This was the most precious gift which Amey gave me in my life. Till today I think, what did I do to win his heart, except shaking his hand every day, in spite of him ignoring me day after day. But this small act of shaking hands could help me receive such big honour. That I Believe is the power of giving.

If you give you will certainly receive either from the same person or from a different person, either in the same form or the other form. The equation is simple:

GIVING = RECEIVING

The more you give, the more you receive as the universe always keeps the balance. There can never be imbalance in the universe.

I would recommend the following practices which will certainly make your life a bit more wonderful and will open all the doors for receiving:

1. Learn to appreciate with honesty and appreciate as many people as many times as you possibly can. Avoid false appreciation, as that will not serve the purpose. Be generous while appreciating.

2. Greet everyone and everything in life with a smile. Right from people to situations.

3. Don't use ordinary or low energy words while talking about others, self or situations. Remember the quality of your communication determines the quality of your life.

4. Offer help if someone needs it.

5. Be calm and think before you speak

6. If you have decided to pay someone then feel good when you do so.

7. Increase the use of these three magical words: Thank you, please and sorry.

8. Forgive and forget the past. Move ahead.

From this moment, start appreciating people, start being the reason for their happiness, start feeding the beggars, start giving as much as possible and you will keep becoming rich, richer and super rich!

Vision Board

It's a board which you hang in a place where it can be seen by you easily and regularly. In the corporate world I have come across people who pin their dreams on the soft board in front of their workstation. Things like their future car, their dream home, their next promotion, a hobby long forgotten or a vacation to their dream destination. Whatever it is, it is imperative that the object of your dream is in front of your eyes in a visual form. Maintain a vision board and give a shape to your dreams. You don't have to spend your entire day thinking about it, but it should be in front of your eyes when you wake up in the morning and when you go to bed at night.

Let it grow on you!

Due to my profession I have the privilege to visit different organizations and companies. When I enter these companies, I feel great as all their walls are painted with their goals and visual reminders about their targets. When I worked with Symantec, I remember that the customer satisfaction survey score targets were close to 80 % and later they increased it to 85%. People disliked it as achieving 80 was a tough task and the company was now talking about 85%. We didn't find them realistic. But the leadership team believed in it and covered all the floors with posters and stickers of 85%. Surprisingly the entire team started achieving these targets in less than 3 months' time. Next year the company raised the targets to 90% and the same story was repeated but everyone was ultimately successful in achieving them.

There are many people who come to me and share, that, after attending my workshop they prepared the vision board and they lost count on how many of those wishes turned into reality without they having to constantly work on them. Vision Board, **It works**!

If you are a person who has dreams but constantly loses hope in them, the vision board will help you focus.

So what are you waiting for! Right this moment take a chart paper and start pasting the images which are close to your dreams. Start creating the blue print of your success. Don't delay this, as the universe loves speed!

Besides Incantation, human beings operate from a very simple concept in whatever task they endeavour. It's called the concept of 'Pain and Pleasure'

Principle of Pain and Pleasure

Behind every action there is this theory of pain and pleasure at work. We work towards pleasure and every pain that we undertake is in anticipation of pleasure in the near future.

This theory of **Pain and Pleasure** is a very powerful concept and at **Challenging Horizons,** we have given it some extra mileage after studying the huge effect it has on people's life.

A few months ago a girl walked up to me for an autograph after a session, when she shared with me that she found my session extremely motivating and inspiring. She also shared, that, she has big dreams in her life and that after listening to me she realizes that she has the power of fulfilling each one of them. But the biggest challenge, she was facing right then was her English language skills. To fulfil her dreams, she says, she will need the help of this language but she probably doesn't even know her basics properly. "After listening to you, I know I can. I definitely can," she said. "But I just need to know, just how to go about it. It's a vast language and I am 24. Will it take me another 24 years to read and learn this language and speak like a Pro? I am trying to learn it, but finding it very difficult. After all it's not my first language. And I have other work too. I don't get sufficient time to invest in it."

I made her sit down then and there, and list down ten painful areas she is facing now for not knowing the language and ten pleasures she will experience if she could speak it fluently. I also asked her to write about what pain she will have to go through in her entire life if she doesn't learn this language in time. I asked her to pause before jotting down every one of the ten points and feel it through as she may also exaggerate her pain and pleasure points while penning it down. She can elaborate on them as much as she wishes. I advised her to take her time.

She did take her time!

Almost an hour to write down those twenty odd points!

She then discussed them with me. We elaborated on the pain she was facing for not knowing the language. We spoke at length the mileage she imagines she will get by learning it. We also took time out to discuss the obstacles she will be facing while going through the learning process that will give her a renewed sense of pain. We pointed out possibilities like time crunch, money crunch, the difficulty in learning a new language, especially when the brain and mouth needs to be trained to modulate new sounds, expressions and tongue movement.

I said to her "There will be an urge to give up, to let go and opt for an easier option."

'But at this moment she will have to remember the—pain that she will incur for a life time—by letting go, to relieve herself from the current pain. At the same time she will have to make the calculation of the pleasure she will experience by braving this little pain'

Just one month down the line, she came to me to say 'thank you'. To my surprise she was not using even a single word of Hindi or Marathi to explain her thoughts. I could see a lot of confidence in her. Yes she was making a few mistakes, while speaking but she was courageous enough to tell the world, that she is learning English. I was very happy and complimented her. Today I use her story, as an example in many of my sessions. She speaks immaculate English today and is on the verge of realizing each one of her dreams!

How did she achieve this? The fact is that the moment her mind made the calculation of pain and pleasure her signals automatically got aligned to the job of attracting pleasure and avoiding pain.

No matter how late we like to wake up in the morning, we never miss an examination that's scheduled in the morning, or miss a scheduled train or flight. Even in our sleep, our sub-conscious mind makes this calculation. Each and every person operates from this instinct, but is not aware of it. So being aware of it and consciously using it to calculate the outcome of your life, goes a long way in achieving your burning desire.

Try talking to some men and women who consciously maintain a beautiful body and love their vital statistics, men and women who love to spend hours in front of the mirror and admire them-selves and like to be admired by others. You will realize that these people not only avoid food and beverages detrimental to their health, they actually hate it. They find the seductive aroma of a juicy piece of meat dripping with extra dollops of cheese and laced with cream obnoxious or sumptuous wedges of potatoes deep fried in oil gastronomically repulsive. They will instead happily fork through a leafy bowl of salad for lunch and tell you how satisfying an apple is for dinner.

Their mind has successfully made the calculation of pain and pleasure and has aligned their signals to it. They automatically shift through things that will give them pain and sub-consciously gets attracted to things of their pleasure.

Human beings do this calculation constantly, and since they are not aware of its existence they are not aware of its effect either. We miscalculate it to short term benefits. We forget to consider the bigger picture and hence fail to fulfil the dreams.

I have just talked about people who have great bodies and have their thought process aligned to the universe. But there are millions of people across the world who aspires to have a good physique. But one day, at the age of sixty they rest their back on a rocking chair, pat their pot belly and wonder where those years have gone when they wanted to look like their favourite movie star. They get surprised by the fact that while their movie star look almost the same, they look old enough to fit into their father character! Their 'one day' in the future never arrived.

That's because their thoughts were not congruent with their desire.

They haven't practiced Incantation. Their thoughts were feeble and they were not supported by correct actions, emotion or thoughts.

They looked at the pleasure but were reluctant to go through the perceived pain. They got daunted by the temporary pain, of changing their habitual diet and their daily routine of exercise. They wanted to look like Tom Cruise or Hrithik Roshan or if they were women, they panted after the perfect vital statistics of Angelina Jolie or Bipasha Basu of Bollywood but it was just a passing thought. Probably they saw Dhoom—2 or Lara Croft and had a spike of desire. They follow it up for a few days with heightened intensity and enthusiasm. They buy new shoes and attire, join a gym and wake up early to rush to the gym. Then slowly, and due to lack of Incantation, their enthusiasm dampens, waking early in the morning becomes a nightmare and training in the gym too tedious.

They don't know how to make the calculation of pain and pleasure. They get bogged down by the temporary pain and keep pushing the pleasure behind.

It's called a Miscalculation.

Don't forget that the sub-conscious mind still does the calculation because it's a natural process. But being unaware of it leads to such miscalculation that topples the total outcome. They give up, initially 'just for 2 days break' and then the two days increases to five, fifteen and fifty till they forget they had any such plans in their life to get back to shape!

Twenty years later they still feel the pain, probably with an increased intensity, because they missed the calculation before or miscalculated it.

Once when I was travelling and got a chance to meet one of the workshop participants who was a handsome hunk with amazing personality and strong built. I asked him 'what the secret of his exceptional fitness is?' What he shared with me was really interesting.

He said 'sir, there was a time when I was very thin. I was in college and I had a classmate whom I liked. We were good friend. I was never able to express my feelings to her. My physique was also the reason behind it. I used to think that I was not good looking. Many people remarked about my thinness and joked about me being a bamboo shaft, were not very exciting. I wanted to work on it. I made plans to exercise many times but could never stick to the schedule. I even took medicines to improve my health but nothing worked. One day this girl, whom I secretly admired, passed a sarcastic comment about my figure, which pinched me a lot and made me uncomfortable. That day I left the college with lot of frustration and to some extent guilt about my own physique. I started going to the gym regularly. I exercised at least 4-5 hours a day and in 3 months time I got a wonderful physique. People slowly started noticing me in college, as I intentionally wore clothes that enhanced my newly attained body and appreciation poured in. Since then I exercise daily and maintain this physique.'

Did you notice how one small remark from a person generated so much pain in his heart. In order to avoid that, he turned his weakness into strength. There are many such stories of that one slap, one insult, one sarcastic remark, one negative word, which motivated many to bring extraordinary changes in their lives. Human mind wants to avoid pain and wants to gain lot of pleasure! Here, this person's mind could perceive insurmountable pain when this girl laughed at him and the mind never wanted to go through it again and hence he got motivated to turn it around.

The right calculation of pain and pleasure can surely help in many areas and some of them are:

1. To make some important decisions which you are unable to make due to fear or ambiguity
2. Motivating self to take the actions which are important for you but you have been procrastinating
3. Relationship enhancement
4. To put a full stop to bad habits
5. To improve the overall quality of life.

Do your pain-pleasure calculation today, now, especially for all those activities which can give you huge returns in life, but you have been pushing due to your laziness or your false assumption of being busy. By learning to do the right calculations about pain and pleasure you will surely be very successful in motivating yourself.

Desired Values with the Demonstrated One

They were just not in the same plane.

Whenever you fail to achieve something, you fail because; somewhere your desired values and demonstration of those values were very different. For an example: many people walk up to me and say 'sir, we want to become good in public speaking, we really want to speak like you in front of a crowd. This is the desire or we can call it the desired value. I tell them that it's easy to become a public speaker. You just need to come, speak and go back to your seat. Rest will be taken care of with time. But not surprisingly, out of the 100 hardly 2 people would actually come up and speak. Meaning, people want to get the fruits but don't want to pay for those fruits. They don't want to take actions, as they are paralyzed by the fear or are caught up in their own comfort zone. You need to work for your desires to turn them into results. If the desire is to earn lot of money, then every action of yours should demonstrate that you are money conscious. If your desire is to be a businessman, then today is the day when you need to take your first step. Don't wait till the situations will become ideal because that time will never come. There will never be an ideal situation. You need to act and act today!

Desired and demonstrated value is a very simple concept that makes the calculation easy and workable. It's like a graph that you can put up in the corner of your vision board to observe and update from time to time. When you can see your progress on the wall in the form of a graph which is measurable, reaching it becomes easy.

How do you make the graph?

If you are maintaining a vision board and you have every parameter added to it, you need to put that part as the desired point in your graph. Go down on your vision board and list your present status. Jot down bullet point on how much work you have done in the direction of achieving your desired object. Put that as your demonstrated value point. Then with each step you take towards your goal draw a line higher and towards the desired value point of your graph. The climb will be fun and since you can see it as a measurable quantity, it will be easier.

You can put in as many parameters as desired to make it more detailed—like a time line, which keeps you on a time track, you can put a time frame to it, a deadline for each milestone to be achieved, and tick it off when the job is done. As you see the graph lines grow longer and closer towards your goal reaching it will be easier. The ineffectiveness will be minimized. Incantation will come easy. And achieving your desired goal will be fun.

MODELLING

When we are on our path of following our heart we usually have a role model in our mind. It's the person's entire personality or a few traits of his that we would like to inculcate in us—like though I do not aspire to become the President of The United States of America, I would surely like to have a 'larger than life' magnetic personality like him. Or even though I do not aspire to become a film star, I would definitely like to have a mastery over language and delivery potential like Amitabh Bacchan. His tone, his godly voice, his intonation, even his body language when he speaks, is hypnotic. Listening to him or watching him when he sits on the high chair and talks to the contestants on KBC is an out-of-the-world experience. We also might have achievements specific personalities like say—someone wants to be a big business magnate like Laxmi Mittal or Dhiru Bhai Ambani. We get inspired by their movie-script like, dramatic style of achievements, from 'Zero-to-Hero' in one life time. Or we want to become an established player like Sachin Tendulkar or Brian Lara.

There is a short cut to do it. Or let's not call it a short-cut. It's a definite and a proven scientific procedure. It comes very handy when we have a target personality in our life and we want to be like them. It's called 'Modelling'.

'Anthony Robins' propagated the theory of NLP in a big way. He says that success leaves clues. Every trait traces a neurological pattern. If we can figure out that pattern, we will become like him. If we have a role model, we need to spend time observing him—the way he walks, the way he talks, his voice modulation, tone of speech, his approach towards a certain situation, his attitude towards people, the way he dresses, the way he grooms himself, his likes, dislikes, everything.

By asking right questions and by studying his patterns of behaviour, you can get a map or let's say a rough sketch of his brain. If you know NLP then it will be easier for you to get this as NLP (Neuro linguistic programming) is the science which helps you to understand how your brain works and how it processes the instructions, situations and commands. Different parts of the brain are responsible for different characteristic of a person. Constantly observing the person and trying to ape him means you are trying to walk in his footsteps. You are tracing his neurological pattern. By trying to copy his external features, some of his thought process too rubs in—For an example if he is wearing a certain brand of shoes and you start doing the same, with time you find reason for liking it, which is more than just aping him. Like maybe it's more comfortable than the shoes you previously wore, and matches with all your trousers and has a longer life span. Then you will probably find justice in preferring the trousers that he wears that compliments his shoes perfectly. You begin to understand a bit more of the tie culture, something you have never worn before. You talk about Lasagnes and discuss at length about white wine and it's appropriateness in respect to occasions. So where exactly is all that leading to? You are modelling him. Some of it, knowingly and some unknowingly.

The more you train yourself to micro-study the concerned person and inculcate all that in yourself, the more accurate your Modelling will be and that will get you closer to the magnitude of his success.

Anthony Robins demonstrated it by experimenting a simple test on the US Army. He asked them to give him their 10 best shooters and he will convert every other shooter like them. He applied NLP practices over them. Asked them hundreds of odd question and most of them had nothing to do with shooting. He then started teaching those behavioural and thinking patterns to the rest of the shooters. Anthony Robins was no shooter himself so he did not take them to the shooting range to train. He did not even speak much about shooting. Instead he concentrated on all aspect of their personalities and made it a 3D approach. At the end of their training, when they were taken to the shooting range they were at par with the best 10. Isn't this a miracle? Actually no! It's science. To be successful you need certain mindset and certain physiological traits. If you get them right you will be successful soon and the easiest way to be successful is to model someone who already is successful.

When I left my job I was clueless as to how will I earn money and how will I setup my business. I had limited money in my pocket. Dreams were big and I was alone. All I had was a burning desire and some hope. I once got a chance to attend a meeting of a group called the Business Networking International. Here entrepreneurs' of different genre meet once a week and discuss business ideas and strategies. They exchange knowledge. They also refer to each other if they come across possibilities of their partners' field.

When I went there for the first time, I rode in a bike wearing jeans and a T-shirt. I saw all the other members wearing business suits, proper formal shoes and discuss business worth millions. At that point of time all I had was one lakh in the bank to survive on and no job. I looked on, as all of them left in their respective cars after the meet was over.

I had to do some real hard thinking. There were fees to be paid for the initial enrolment; there were some charges for weekly meetings and then some nominal amount to be paid for official parties that was conducted every week. Though the situations were not in favour but I decided to be a part of this group, as I knew that I will be able to extract some good things from here for sure. On top of that I had a good amount of knowledge of NLP and hence I had trust in modelling. I started thinking about this group and finally handed over the cheque of Rs 25000 against my enrolment. I knew what I was risking, but I also knew the power of modelling!

For the next meeting itself I invested in my wardrobe and borrowed my friend's car. While on the first occasion I shied away from the discussions of lakhs and crores, this time, I deliberately got involved and took initiatives. I observed each one of them carefully in the lines of NLP and tried to inculcate them in me. It sure made me feel different from the usual 'ME'. Initially it was like I was putting on an act. But slowly the act became me. I started getting comfortable with it and there was more. Where I was not sure, if I will be able to start up on my own or not, after attending BNI and interacting with all those established people I started thinking of not only making a success story of it, I too started thinking in terms of lakhs and crores . . . got myself comfortable with terms like 'yearly turnover', 'sharing best practice' and 'monthly target'. It became less scary for me to take big business decisions, where big money was involved and big thoughts, much bigger than I was capable of at that time. With time it got under my skin. *I practiced modelling.*

Today I am where they were that day and whose ways I had inculcated. In fact some of them are my clients today, trying to learn ways of expanding their wealth and business.

SWITCH WORDS

Wouldn't it be great to have a magic wand that you could just wave at any situation or creative project, and have it turn out beneficially just as you wish?

Actually, we all have such a wand! However, most of us are not aware of it, and have never received an instruction manual for its use. (So I write one!)

Your Word is Your Magic Wand

Your word is your wand. Intentional creative thoughts bring about intentional desired results.

Intentional creative thoughts can take the form of images or words, or both. We can envision an image and be grateful about it like it has already materialised, or we can declare or affirm a beneficial condition or state of affairs, in words and be grateful in the same manner. Or we can do both image and text together.

The affirmations or declarations that most people use are complete sentences, but a pioneer named 'James Mangan' in the past century identified about a hundred specific single words that are extraordinarily effective when used as an intentional creative thought, to bring about a specific desired result.

Using a single word to create with, instead of a long sentence (as in conventional affirmations or creative declarations), brings a greatly increased laser-like focus of your creative energy in this single moment of now.

Introducing "Switch Words"

James Mangan called these special words "Switch Words." A "Switch Word" is the essence of an experience, condition, or desired result, expressed as a single word. Declare, affirm, chant, sing, or even just mentally "intend" the Switch Word, and like turning on a lamp with a switch, the desired result appears.

For an example: one of the most practically useful ones is: REACH.— to find anything you're looking for, such as

- Misplaced items in the physical world (keys, papers, tools, etc.);
- Forgotten ideas or information in your mind or memory (names, numbers, etc);
- Solutions to problems.

Whenever you misplace something, or searching for something or you want to solve a problem, just persistently declare or chant, silently or aloud, "REACH." Then let yourself go wherever you feel to, and watch yourself go directly to what you are looking for! Some aspect of your being knows where it is, and "REACH" reliably makes the connection! Try it . . . it really works! Very useful in everyday life!

Similarly . . .

- Whenever you want to sell something, say: GIVE.
- Whenever you want to make money: COUNT.
- Whenever you want to make something beautiful: CURVE.
- For good health, and/or for peace: BE.
- To work miracles or for extraordinary accomplishment: DIVINE.

And about 90 more such Switch Words for other specific purposes! Plus one master-key Switch Word to do anything with mastery: TOGETHER.

Using Switch Words, you can easily enjoy increased creative power, effectiveness, accomplishment, fun, prosperity, aliveness, togetherness, life mastery, and life satisfaction.

YOU CAN FIND THE ENTIRE LIST OF SWITCH WORDS ON THE INTERNET. THEY ARE VERY POWERFUL SO SEARCH FOR YOUR OWN BENEFIT AS TO HOW THESE CAN CHANGE YOUR ENTIRE LIFE.

Spread Love and Joy Around

"The future, higher evolution will belong to those who live in joy, who share joy, and who spread joy."

—Torkom Saraydarian

Joy, as the energy of love, which is the highest vibration on this planet. Everything in the universe is energy; it can be measured and reduced to vibrational frequencies. It's a universal law that as we think and feel, we vibrate, and as we vibrate we attract. When we are in the high joy vibration, we attract what is for our greater good.

The Ancient Egyptians saw Joy as a sacred responsibility. They believed that upon their death, the God Osiris would ask them two questions: "Did you bring Joy?" and "Did you find Joy?" Those who answered 'yes' could continue their journey into the afterlife.

For at least the next week or two, ask yourself these two questions each and every day: Did I bring joy? Did I find joy?

"Man loves because he is Love. He seeks Joy, for he is Joy. He thirsts for God for he is composed of God and he cannot exist without Him."

—Sathya Sai Baba

Now the biggest problem you may face is that—How to bring joy to others and to be joyful always?

So what do you think you should do to bring and spread joy?

Though I need not tell you much here about this as you have done it a lot when you were kids and you just need to recall your childhood days. If this is difficult then spend some time with kids and watch and observe them carefully, you will again start developing this muscle as it's very easy.

Yes become kids again, do everything to bring that energy and enthusiasm again. Dance and Sing the way you want to, jump whenever you feel like, laugh as loudly as possible, live in the moment and have as much fun as possible. Don't suppress your emotions, rather express them, let them come out. Just flow with the flow. Master the art of living in the moment and joy and love would be all around.

MEDITATION

On one level, meditation is a tool. It can help combat stress, fosters physical health, helps with chronic pain, can make you sleep better, feel happier, be more peaceful, as well as be present. But on a deeper level, meditation is a doorway into the unknown. It can help us get a sense of the mystery of who we are.

When you start meditating, you will notice how unruly the mind is. I remember being quite shocked by this! I noticed that my mind was all over the place. Profound thoughts about my past or future jostled with mundane thought clips about what groceries I needed to buy. Sometime later I would notice that I had spent 15 minutes running a painful memory over and over. It was like sitting in a crazy cinema!

So, if you're starting out with meditation, please don't beat yourself up about your wild mind. It is a natural condition. In time you will learn to work kindly with the barrage of thoughts and you will find some clarity and peacefulness.

Here are some simple tips on how to start meditating.

Posture: Whether you sit on a chair or cross-legged on the floor, make sure that your spine is upright with head up. If you are slumped your mind will drift. Mind and body are intertwined. If your body is well-balanced, your mind will also balance in time. To straighten up, imagine that your head is touching the sky.

Eyes: Try and keep your eyes open. Open eyes allow you to be more present. Just lower your eyes and let your gaze be short. If you close your eyes you will be more likely to drift away on thoughts and stories. However, it's important to do what is comfortable for you. Some people find closing their eyes much more effective. It's good to experiment and see what feels best for you.

Focus: In ordinary consciousness we are hardly ever present. For an example, sometimes we drive the car while being preoccupied with thoughts. Suddenly we arrive at our destination and don't remember anything about the drive!

So, meditation is a wonderful way of waking up to our life. Otherwise we miss most of our experiences because we are somewhere else in our mind! Let's take a look at what focus is. In ordinary life, we tend to equate focus with concentration. That's like using the mind like a concentrated beam of light. But in meditation, that kind of mind isn't helpful. It's too sharp and edgy. To focus in meditation means to pay soft attention to whatever you place in the centre of awareness. I suggest using the breath as a focus. It's like a natural door that connects 'inside' and 'outside'. Zen Master Toni Packer says:

Attention comes from nowhere. It has no cause. It belongs to no one.

Breathing: Paying attention to breathing is a great way to anchor you in the present moment. Notice your breath streaming in and out. There's no need to regulate the breath—just let it be natural.

Counting Your Breath: If you have difficulty settling, you can try counting your breath. This is an ancient meditation practice. On your outbreath, silently count "one", then "two", and up to "four". Then return to "one". Whenever you notice your thoughts have strayed far away or you find yourself counting "thirty three", simply return to "one". In this way, "one" is like coming home to the present moment. It's good to return without a backward glance.

Thoughts: When you notice thoughts, gently let them go by returning your focus to the breath. Don't try and stop thoughts; this will just make you feel agitated. Imagine that they are unwelcome visitors at your door: acknowledge their presence and politely ask them to leave. Then shine the soft light of your attention on your breath.

Emotions: It's difficult to settle into meditation if you are struggling with strong emotions. This is because some emotions tend to breed stories in the mind. Especially anger, shame and fear creates stories that repeat over and over in the mind. Anger and shame make us keep looking at past events. Fear looks at the future with stories that start with, "What if . . ."

The way to deal with strong emotions in meditation is to focus on the body feelings that accompany the emotion. For an example, this could be the tight band of fear around the chest or the hot rolling of anger in the belly. Let go of the stories and refocus on your body. In this way you are honouring your emotions but not becoming entangled in stories.

Silence: Silence is healing. I know that there is a lot of 'meditation music' around, but nothing beats simple silence. Otherwise the music or sounds on the tape just drown out the chatter in your mind. When we sit in silence we actually get to experience what our mind is doing. There is steadiness and calmness that comes from sitting in silence.

In time, outer and inner silence meet and you come to rest in the moment.

Duration: Start with 10 minutes and only sit longer if you feel that it's too short. Don't force yourself to meditate longer if you are not ready to do that. In time you might like to extend your meditation to 25 minutes. That's a length that allows you to settle your mind without causing too much stress on your body. Most importantly, shrug off any 'shoulds'. Some people enjoy sitting for an hour at a time. Others find that they can't sit longer than 10 minutes. Do what feels right for you!

Place: It's lovely to create a special place to sit. You can even make a shrine or an altar that you can face when you sit in meditation. You might like to place a candle on your altar and objects that have meaning to you. It's lovely to find objects for your altar as you walk. Maybe you find stones, or seashells, or flowers that speak to you.

Enjoyment: Most of all it's important to enjoy meditation. You might like to try sitting with a hint of a smile. Be kind to yourself. Start sitting just a little each day. It's helpful to establish a daily habit.

Take Risks

Life is a lot like a poker game. Players put down their money and take a chance at either winning the jackpot or losing their shirts. There are both, an element of luck and skill involved, but essentially it all comes down to what you're willing to risk.

But let's roll back things a bit and examine the people who simply watch the game. They're not willing to put the risk involved to see what happens. And that's where the metaphor ends. You have a choice about playing poker, the game of life though is much different.

Taking Important Risks

If life is really like a game, then the key difference would be that you really don't have a choice in whether you want to play it or not. It's one big table and everyone has a seat. So either you play it by grabbing the horns or allow someone else to play it for you. The choice is yours!

In fact, I think of life and risk as the same thing. Everything about life is a risk. You could get into an accident or become ill at any moment. These are the everyday risks that we got used to and so do not think of them as risks at all!

Most people live the mundane life. Like they have a seat at the poker table and so they sit it out. But to make life sharp and live it with some value, risks will be involved. The results that you will get upon taking those risks will make life worthwhile.

These risks can bring you pain when they go wrong which is why most people avoid them. But these people hardly have dreams to dream or the nerves to fulfil them.

So when we talk about risks, we will omit them for decency sake. We will not disturb them. We will let them have their seats, while the others can pick up their glasses and follow life.

The five important risks in life are:

Caring about someone else:

And why do we call it a risk? This is because; it can be emotionally very taxing. If you've ever gone through a bad break up or dissolved a friendship, you know exactly how heart-breaking it can be. But it's worth the risk a thousand folds because the experience one goes through, when you love someone is something that cannot be replaced by anything else in this world.

Letting another person get close to you and caring about them deeply can be a scary thing. It would be so simple for them to break your trust and hurt you. But the beauty behind letting someone get close to you is that you get to know each other deeply and your bond together is tightly woven. That can be a great feeling.

Learning and trying new things: There's always an element of risk when you're trying something new. Starting a new activity like rock-climbing or surfing can be scary at first, but a large part of the fun is overcoming that fear.

The same goes for big life changes. If you want to go to a grad school or move to another part of the world, you have to just jump in and do it. It's impossible to do these incredible things without accepting a little bit of risk.

Following your passions and dreams: How many people's dreams have been squashed before they ever got off the ground? It's a sad, but true statement that most people never take their dream past the planning stage. Everyone should follow their dreams no matter how unlikely they seem to be.

I started following my dreams because of a simple thought: when else am I going to do them? You can't wait for things to happen to you. And it's not as if you have another life waiting for you after you die. So the best time to pursue your dreams will always be right now.

Failing: The downside of taking risks is that there is always a chance of failure. Otherwise they'd be known as sure-things. Of course failure remains the biggest obstacle for people to take those risks, but it shouldn't stop you.

I've read that big companies in Silicon Valley will often pass over their own people for promotion to hire people who had started up companies that later went bankrupt. Apparently, they like the guts of people who will risk bankruptcy and failure. That's a good lesson for life in general.

Your viewpoints: Everyone has a view of what's going on in the world and how things work. Expressing how you feel can be risky since you don't know how people will react. You might find some people will be hostile to your opinions. You might even find that your opinion is misplaced.

Many people are content to just sit on the side-lines and refuse to stand up to share their viewpoint. But you can't be afraid of saying how you feel just because it might be unpopular or wrong. People who are making the most out of their lives have unique opinions and insights into things. A big part of living life fully comes, in being able to express those points of view.

Risks are Necessary for a Nourishing Life

I can definitely see life as a game and the risks we take are just the ante we use to play it. And even though taking risks means you might fail from time to time, it is better than not taking any risks and living life below your potential.

Besides, when you see life as a game it changes your whole attitude about winners and losers. Games work best when even those who lose, have fun. If you think big successful names does not have a bounty of failure in their kitty, think again. It might just as well surprise you to discover that they actually have more number of failures than you do! Why? Probably because they took more number of risks than you ever did. And treated each failure as a blessed experience—used it as a trampoline, and bounced higher. You might as well start taking risks and see what you're capable of. Otherwise, you're just sitting at the table watching life play out in front of you.

Here are the top 10 ways to take positive risks in your life

1. **Decide what you want and then define and take the biggest risk you can think of which will move you closer to your**

goal. (Taking action towards doing what you want to do is not a risk).

2. **Make a step by step plan towards an important goal and define risks you MUST take to move forward.** (Living a status quo life will not change any situation for which you are stuck)

3. **Ask yourself what is possible and then make a list.** (Most people spend too much time pondering over things that won't work and as a result, justify why taking no action is the best choice)

4. **Take action—do something off the track to create movement towards a goal which is important to you.** (Automatically all that is unnecessary and no longer fits in will crumble.)

5. **Only strive to accomplish few really important things each day.** (Life isn't about having the biggest to-do list) but making progress and living a life which is most important, is actually living it!

6. **Work to develop the relationships which matter to you.** (Don't be afraid to terminate the relationships which no longer work for you or be afraid to pursue new ones which nourish you)

7. **Re-define yourself by WHO you are vs. WHAT you do.** (Job titles are for the human resources staff)

8. **Define and live your perfect vocational day.** (Recreate a life which works better for you vs. one which works better for someone else who really doesn't care about your welfare)

9. **Be your own best friend.** (Easier said than done since people tend to be their own worst critics)

10. **Give yourself permission to take risks in your life.** (Otherwise, you will wait a very long time and then wonder later why change took so long, or worst still—why nothing changed at all)

Taking risks towards what you want in your life is all relevant. What might seem like a big risk to one person might not seem any risk at all to another. Happiness in life, work and relationships comes from the knowledge that you were not afraid to try something new in your life when the status quo no longer worked. Take a few risks towards what you want—Your life will be richer a full circle 360 degree.

Carry Your Divine Stone and Plant a Tree

This sure helps, on your way to success. Take a walk in the morning along the path and look out for a nice little piece of stone. Look at it intensely and give it power. If you would like to follow a ritual and touch the stone to your chosen God, you can do it, but you need to believe in it and its power. Make it yours . . .

DIVINE STONE . . .

It should be small enough to fit into your fist but not tinier than that. Now every time you face a hurdle in your life hold the stone tight in your closed fist and feel its divine power seeping into you. Believe that it gives you the power to solve all problems. Energize it so much that it is all powerful. If you can, accumulate all your powers and put it into the stone. This will give you lots of strength in the time of crisis. Not just in the time of crisis but every time you make a resolution or do Incantation hold the stone in your fist and feel it. It will help you focus. All your attention will be pinned to that stone. So every time you touch the stone it will activate you and bring you closer to the realization of your dream.

PLANT A TREE . . .

Make that your wish tree and water it every day. As you watch your tree grow so will your fortune. While planting the tree, place a silver coin at the bottom. It attracts positive energy. It will give a plus-plus to your positive signals as well and boost your fortune.

Don't take it as a negative signal if the tree dies. It means nothing. Go and get yourself another sapling and this time try and take care of it. Don't just leave it in the sun to go crisp and die. Observe it every day. Spend 2-3 minutes with it every day and concentrate on its growth, its lush green leaves, the juicy branches, and the sheathed new leaf and feel life flow. Preferably do it in the morning once you wake up from your sleep. It will give momentum to your fortune.

And there is one more thing to be done. Write a

SCRIPT OF YOUR LIFE

This is a process, exactly the way script writers of movies write. Follow the flow—

1) **A purpose of your life.** Why do you want to make your film? The mood of it, the genre that you want it to belong to! Like will it be a comedy, a light hearted abandoned style movie or a grave one with lots of lessons in it or an out and out tragedy or maybe just a love story of the fairy tale kind. The purpose of this movie or let's say the purpose of your life.

2) **A one liner.** This is one line without any full stop. This line will be a condensed form of your entire life. How you would like to perceive your life or how would you want people and your loved ones to remember you. That one thing that will make you happy!

3) **An outline rough sketch.** Here you will roughly jot down, how you would want your various aspects of life to look like. For an example—Academics—hobbies say painting etc.—Masters from B-School—Career in training—First painting exhibition—my first car—3 bedroom apartment in Lokhandwala—get married— Honeymoon in Paris—a world tour—deep sea diving—etc.

4) **Here you will detail your script.** You will pick up each and every pointer in your outlined sketch and elaborate on it with every possible detail like the name of the B-school you are aspiring for, the make and model of that car and the girl probably whom you want to marry one day.

Point number three here will be a very important exercise because the more accurate you are in jotting down that point the more you will be able to keep yourself on track. Your Vision board will look all the more promising, colourful and full of dimensions. Point four, which is the entire script of your life, will be detailed and long. You will spend as many pages as you want for every aspect, down to the colour of the bathroom tile to the name of your children and maybe the agency that famous to facilitate deep sea diving or few best hotel accommodations you would like to board in for your honeymoon.

5) **The conclusion of your script.** It maybe your retirement plan. Or a new venture altogether. Or maybe something very different from what you have been doing for so many years.

It will be so good to not have the government of your country or the organization you work for decide your retirement plan. Instead you do it. You plan when you had enough of action, lived your full quota of life, fulfilled all your dreams and aspirations and want to take some rest. Maybe devote full time on a long forgotten hobby or pick up a new one just for fun ... or relive once again the full circle of your childhood with your grandchildren! Like a movie script or the conclusion of a movie make it nice and beautiful. Plan your last league magnificently. Give people a reason to smile when they think of you.

Thumb rules for writing the script—

No negative words or expressions

And

No past or future tense

Everything comes in present. You write it as if everything has become a reality. I know that might be a grammatical horror but let's do it—for the sake of our own life! We will display our grammatical abilities somewhere else! Everything should be in the present tense. Like—Today I am a trainer in this capacity and I am very happy and I have this new car . . . etc.

Don't say negative things like 'I don't want to stay in India or work in Gurgaon'. Say instead 'I want to stay in UK and work in London.'

Example of a great script which is written by one of my colleagues:

"Hurray! I have got the best life I could ever imagine. I am the happiest, greatest and the best. I get everything very easily in life and I am able to enjoy every moment of it. Life is beautiful. It's colourful and it's full of happiness. I am loving it! Now I am a CEO of a company and in my presence the company is making progress by leaps and bounds. I have received awards for the most innovative CEO, CEO of the Year and Leader of the century. People look up to me with great trust and respect.

I look very handsome and people admire me for my wonderful physique. I hit the gym regularly and I exercise with enthusiasm. I am highly energetic and celebrate every moment of my life."

Few pointers to remember:

1. The script should be full of life. It should have emotions in it and should have feelings associated with it.
2. Imagine as if you have already achieved everything and you are writing the story post your achievements. Don't' write about the process of achieving the things—let the universe decide the process. It knows better than you.

RECORD YOUR SCRIPT

After you have finished writing your script the next step is to read it with feelings and emotions and record it. You must be wondering—why recording it.

Recording is important, especially because of the next step in the process. And the next step is to let this recording play throughout the night while you sleep.

The reason is because when you are sleeping your conscious mind is also sleeping. But the beauty is that your subconscious mind never sleeps. When this recording is played the entire night it directly programs your subconscious mind for better success as it's not bound by those filters which conscious mind applies before the things can get into the subconscious. This is the reason I always recommend this activity as one of the most powerful one. This has the power to shift your entire life and real quick time too!

My parents and I were searching for a good match for my sister. The hunt was now on for almost 5 years. We were all unhappy and exhausted. We did not know what to do. One fine day, while having a telephonic conversation with my parents, they sounded piercingly worried and listless. I was in Pune, around 1300 kilo-meters away from them. I felt pathetic. I cried, and when I got tired of crying, I went off to sleep. Next morning when I woke up, I decided to take charge of the situation. The first thing which I did that day was to make my script. I wrote in that script about all those things which I had in my mind about my sister's marriage day. I wrote the story as if she is getting married in front of my eyes. I recorded and it kept playing it the whole night. Nothing significant happened for the next 14 days but the 15th day I could witness the miracle of this entire process.

I could find an eligible match from a matrimonial website and asked my father to check with them. My father went and found that person suitable and a good match. Now it was their turn to visit us and meet my sister. I again wrote a script well in advance about what will happen when they come and how they would react after meeting my sister.

To my surprise everything went in the same way, as in my script. Today my sister is happily married and things went as per my script.

Till today I am surprised that, how the things shifted in less than 15 days. I don't deny the fact that it could have been a coincidence. Some may even call it destiny. But my question is that:

WHY AND HOW THE DESTINY BECAME FAVORABLE EVERYTIME I WROTE THE SCRIPT? WHY NOT BEFORE THAT? WHY THE THINGS DIDN'T CHANGE OVERNIGHT IN THOSE AREAS ABOUT WHICH I HAVE NOT WRITTEN THE SCRIPT?

I could understand the fact that when the subconscious mind is programmed well, then everything can go well. This is why it's said that a child's 70% programming happens till the age of 7 years as till that time the conscious mind is not fully developed and the things are getting recorded in the subconscious mind.

It's just the one time effort. If you follow it you can get huge benefits. It's very simple to do:

1. Write your script with passion
2. Record it
3. Let it play the whole night

Now I do it for almost everything and guess what—I am living the life which I wanted and which I always dreamt of.

So what are you waiting for, close the book and write the script. Write it with lot of positivity, write it in present tense and make it fun to listen to if possible.

ACT NOW

It's good to know the rules of life and the laid down short cuts of the society to lead a nice and preferably easy life. But people who are remembered today are remembered because they broke through the armour of the so called conventional life and etched a path of their own.

So live well and don't strangulate your imagination. Remember, it is these very beautiful dreams and imaginations of yours that make the world.

"The intellect has little to do on the road of discovery. There comes a leap in consciousness, call it intuition or what you will, and the solution comes to you, and you don't know how or why."

> *"I am enough of an artiste to draw freely upon my imagination. Imagination is more important than knowledge. Knowledge is limited. Imagination encircles the world." ALBERT EINSTEIN*

In these few pages I have shared enough to make you aware of the immense power of the mind and its unique features. Mind Power is a vast subject and inexhaustible. But since the day I have started writing it, I am finding it difficult to stop. IGNITING THE SPARK though stops here. Through this book I have shared with you the punch of this program of mine which is incidentally my signature program. The one that I started my life with, got hooked to and couldn't stop the miracles in my life that it created. So there will be some more and that's a promise. This book is just the beginning of a great journey. I had a wonderful time writing it and I believe you had a great time too with me through this extraordinary journey.

So if this book has motivated you to go on a more deeper, more intense and magnanimous celestial trip of the mind, tighten your seat belts and cruise through. And what luggage do you carry with you on this bizarre trip? Your truth! Pure intention! Undiluted attention and your honesty! Remember, the Universe grants wishes to only those people who connect with it honestly, because there is no way one can cheat nature.

Friends any new idea, learning or awareness is absolutely great and absolutely useless if not put to use. It's like we all know that if we go to the gym and exercise, jog, weight train, swim, do yoga, follow a diet etc. we will have a great body. But just knowing it is not good enough. Slouching on a bean bag in front of the TV with a bowl of deep fried potato wafers and a bulging paunch resting on a meaty thigh will not help you achieve that great body even with that score and score of knowledge you have. Going out instead and doing the needful will!

Hence knowing the Power of the Mind through all the pages of this book is great, but then ignoring this knowledge the moment you complete reading the last page and close the book, will not help. You will have to take it to the gym—the mind gym. Work it out. The exercises are skilfully designed by experts and time proven to give your mind the required curves and immense muscular power. Reading it and refreshing it from time to time will pump it up and keep the high-wax shine!

Someone has rightly said that—if you keep on doing the same thing which you have been doing in the past then you will keep getting the same results which you have been getting or may be getting less. I know you have been getting the results in your life so far, but wouldn't it excite you if you could achieve few more things in the same time span with the same resources and with less effort. I am sure it would.

Most techniques which I have shared in this book are not going to cost you money or too much of your efforts. You may dislike some activities and you may not believe in few things. My advice is that whether you believe in them or not—is there any harm in giving it a shot? From my experience of dealing with thousands of people I can say with confidence that each technique has the power to bring a revolution in your entire life. Be wise and act wise.

You have got only one life. Only one person is standing between you and your success and that is you. Learn to get out of your own ways and you will see life will offer you those treasures which you would never have even imagined for yourself.

SO GO FLY HIGH IN THE SKY, FLOW WITH THE FLOW, PLAY THAT GAME WHICH EXCITES YOU THE MOST, TAKE THOSE DECISIONS WHICH HAS BEEN PENDING FOR LONG, ACCEPT THOSE BIG CHALLENGES WHICH SCARED YOU, DARE TO TAKE THOSE LEAPS WHICH YOU AVOIDED IN THE PAST, SING THAT SONG WHICH YOU ALWAYS WANTED TO, DANCE THE WAY YOU FEEL LIKE, HUG THOSE WHO DESERVE, ASK FOR FORGIVENESS TO WHOM YOU HAVE HURT, APPRECIATE THOSE WHO DESERVE IT THE MOST, LOVE YOURSELF, SHATTER

THOSE BARRIERS WHICH YOU HAVE CREATED FOR YOURSELF, BREAK FREE FROM ALL LIMITATIONS WHICH YOU HAVE CREATED, THINK—THINK BIG, TAKE MASSIVE LEAPS OF FAITH AND THEN YOU WILL SEE THE ENTIRE WORLD WILL BE WITH YOU. TODAY IS THE DAY. LIVE IT TO THE FULLEST AS YOU NEVER KNOW WHETHER TOMORROW WILL COME OR NOT.

YOU AND ONLY YOU CAN TAKE YOURSELF TO THE TOP. NO OTHER PERSON. YOU ARE THE GOD AND GOD IS YOU. YOU ARE THE UNIVERSE AND THE UNIVERSE IS YOU RECOGNIZE THAT POWER, HONOR THAT STRENGTH, CREATE THE MASTER PIECE OUT OF YOURSELF.

Live with Love, Live with Passion, Live with excitement and enjoy every moment. All the very best!

About Mr. Bhupendra Singh Rathore (BSR)

Hi, This is Bhupendra Singh Rathore. You may also address me as BSR. My mission is to help you and your team achieve preeminence—that's where you become the benchmark by which all others are judged. It's where you play at such a level that you set the standard for your industry or category. It is achievable. In fact, it's necessary. If we're not defining the standard, then someone else is and they are going to enjoy the rewards of being the best. And by the way, either we become the best, or we become irrelevant. There is no middle ground.

These are extreme times. We're all being subjected to extraordinary stress and scrutiny by everyone around us—our colleagues, our clients, and our communities. Good enough isn't good enough any more. Even great may not be good enough. The Pursuit of Preeminence is the only path that will deliver the results that you desire and deserve.

So what are my credentials that qualify me to coach you on your path to preeminence?

Since Feb 2008, I have helped over 200 companies bring out the best in their people so their people could bring out their best for their customers. And I would love to do the same for you and your team.

In 2002, I graduated in commerce and learnt about computers and worked with various MNCs like—**Colgate Palmolive, Convergys, HCL, IBM and Symantec**. During this time I learnt a lot from the corporates and about the corporate world. Somewhere I found that something was missing and I was not very happy working. I was trying to find that missing link and hence I attended many seminars and met many masters. Everyone said—Bhupendra Learn to Follow Your Heart. I also learnt that all I need is within me now and everything is possible in this world. This gave me a new dimension of thinking. I left my well paid job and launched my own training and motivation company, **Challenging Horizons Pvt Ltd** in the year 2008.

Over the next six years, I trained & coached more than **100 thousand** people including entrepreneurs, business leaders & executives. Some of the leaders and executives I have served are from the topmost companies like—**Mercedes Benz, JCB, Thermax, Vodafone, Forbes Marshal, Lear Corporation, Vodafone, Tata Technologies, Mubea Engineering, Tata Teleservices, Federal Bank, Foseco, HP** and many more. To be able coach people and help them systematically I learnt about **NLP, Psychometric Assessments, Coaching Practices, Hypnotherapy, Spirituality, Leadership** Lessons & Various Management Practices. My experiences of building, growing and sustaining a business and leading people have been the true guide. I published one book called **"Dive Within"** to help people understand their hidden powers and potentials. My life's purpose now is to "Create a positive transformation in Individuals & organizations to enable them to reach their true potential for the benefit of society at large".

Today, I am one of India's preeminent coaches and motivators. In the last 12 months, I have delivered over 170 programs to 60 organizations in 19 cities in India. Almost every working day, I am speaking to an organization somewhere in the country. I live to speak and I speak to live. Helping people understand what they are capable of and making them realize who they are is what excites me. Every program is my most important program. I deliver every one as though it could be my last because one day I will be right. I make every session a once-in-a-lifetime experience for my delegates. I immerse them in the insights and distinctions that accelerate their path to preeminence. They laugh. They share. They talk. They have fun. I believe that life is theatre with consequences and no-one ever bored anyone into doing anything. That's why people leave my sessions with the purpose and passion to win, enjoy and make a huge difference.

In case you want to know more about me then I suggest let's connect and I would be more than happy to share whatever you want to know.

But don't just take my word for it. Check out what some of the world's best organizations have to say about my contribution to their success.

Also check out my range of programs. I will customize the right one in the right way to thrill and delight your people.

Call me on **+91** 9011050332 and let's talk about how I can help you excite your people into becoming the best while they help everyone around them do the same. You can also email me @ bsr@ challenginghorizon.com. You may also connect me at various social media platforms and the links are as follows:

Linked In—http://www.linkedin.com/in/BreakthroughWithBSR
Facebook—www.facebook.com/BhupendraSR
YouTube—http://www.youtube.com/BreakthroughWithBSR
Twitter—www.twitter.com/Bhupendra_SR
Websites—www.BSRathore.com | www.DiveWithinByBSR.com

I look forward to our conversation. Until then, remember: Think Big. Take Action and Believe in Yourself.

Lots of Love,

BSR

Welcome to the world of 'Challenging Horizons'

At Challenging Horizons We *Believe* that **Implementable Training & Learning** Increases *Productivity & Transforms Lives*

Our Core Purpose is "Creating a *positive transformation* in individuals & organizations to *enable* them to reach their *true potential* for the benefit of the society at large"

Why CH?

- A Visionary Organization
- Core Focus is on Implementation
- E-Learning | Re-Learning facility for Effective training delivery
- End to End Solutions on the L&D space
- Multiple Industry Experience (Services, Telecom, Manufacturing, Automobile, Retail, FMCG, White goods, BFSI, IT-ITES-BPO, Education, Import Export, SME among Others)
- Exclusive Content Development and Research Team

Contact us if you want to create huge breakthrough and visible results in the following area:

* Leadership Coaching & Training * Sales Trainings & Consulting
* Business Coaching & Consulting * Entrepreneurs Success Solutions
* Life Coaching & Counseling * Key note speeches/Pep Talks
* Other Behavioural / Soft Skills Trainings for Institutions,
Individuals, Entrepreneurs & Corporates

www.challenginghorizon.com |info@challenginghorizons.com
Call us @ +91 9011050332, + 91 9637413838